Oliver Erichson Janson

Notes and descriptions of a few injurious farm and fruit insects of South Africa

Oliver Erichson Janson

Notes and descriptions of a few injurious farm and fruit insects of South Africa

ISBN/EAN: 9783744748827

Printed in Europe, USA, Canada, Australia, Japan

Cover: Foto ©Andreas Hilbeck / pixelio.de

More available books at **www.hansebooks.com**

NOTES AND DESCRIPTIONS

OF A FEW

INJURIOUS FARM & FRUIT INSECTS

OF

SOUTH AFRICA.

COMPILED BY

ELEANOR A. ORMEROD, F. R. Met. Soc., &c.,

Consulting Entomologist of the Royal Agricultural Society of England, and Hon. Member of the Farmers' Club; Hon. & Corr. Mem. of Roy. Ag. and Hort. Soc., S. Australia; Hon. Mem. of Ent. Soc. of Ontario, and Corr. Mem. of Field Nat. Club of Ottawa, Canada; Member of Eastern Province Naturalists' Soc., Cape Colony, &c.

WITH

DESCRIPTIONS AND IDENTIFICATIONS OF THE INSECTS

BY

OLIVER E. JANSON, F.E.S.

———◆———

SIMPKIN, MARSHALL & CO., STATIONERS' HALL COURT.

—

1889.

" I strongly feel that no time can be ill spent which is devoted to the investigation of any subject that bears upon the culture of the land, and is likely to aid in multiplying the produce and benefiting the producer."—JOHN CURTIS, *in Introduction to 'Farm Insects.'*

PREFACE.

To those readers who may care to look over the pages of this little book I should like to offer a few observations as to the reasons for its compilation, and also by way of explanation of why in some cases a fairly full history of the insects referred to is given, together with means of prevention, and a figure accompanying, and in others only a figure and description, or perhaps only the name.

About four years ago Mr. S. D. Bairstow, President of the East Province Natural History Society of Cape Colony, who had whilst in England been one of the contributors to my Annual Reports of 'Observations of Injurious Insects,' wrote to enquire whether, if I was furnished with similar notes regarding pests of the crops in East Province, Cape Colony, I would publish them similarly.

At that time there was not the opportunity which there now is of procuring sound and clear directions for treatment of insect as well as other attacks of crop and stock, by reference to the Editor of the 'Agricultural Journal' published by the Department of Agriculture of Cape Colony;* therefore I willingly

* The 'Agricultural Journal,' published by the Department of Agriculture of the Cape Colony, is issued fortnightly, and is sent gratis to every farmer who is a member of an Agricultural Society or Farmers' Association. Those not entitled to receive the paper gratuitously may

agreed to do my best in case trustworthy agricultural observations could be procured, and specimens of the insects referred to also sent for identification.

Specimens of about fifty kinds of insects were sent over, of which a few proved to be of hitherto undescribed species; and some notes of observation also were sent, but (after a lapse of some time) it proved almost impossible to procure further observation suitable for the kind of agricultural report which my South African correspondents wished me to endeavour to form.

It appeared, however, a great pity not to make as much use as possible of the information which had been sent over, and therefore in the following pages I have given, as far as I can, figures and observations of habits, and means of prevention of some of the pests, and descriptions by which they might be identified. Where nothing further could be given, the name alone has been inserted.

For the identification of the insects sent, and for the descriptions of almost all, I have been indebted—as I have noted on the title-page—to Mr. Oliver E. Janson.

To identify these trustworthily, and to ascertain which were previously unknown, required a knowledge of foreign insects, and likewise a knowledge of the bibliography of the subject, which I do not myself possess, and also much consultation in cases of un-

obtain it on application to Messrs. RICHARDS & SONS, Government Printers, Cape Town; subscription two shillings and sixpence a year. Contribution is invited, to be addressed to the Secretary for Agriculture (the Editor of the Journal), Cape Town.

described species. I therefore beg to acknowledge that for this part of the book I am indebted to the co-operation of Mr. Janson, and to join to my thanks to himself my acknowledgment and thanks also to the scientific specialists who kindly gave their assistance in cases of difficulty. To M. Signoret (Paris), by whose recent decease entomological science has suffered such a severe loss, I am indebted for identification of *Icerya purchasi* and *Lecanium hesperidum;* to M. Bigot (Paris). for confirmation of the *Hippobosca Struthionis* as being a species previously undescribed; to Dr. J. S. Baly, for identification of *Dibolia intermedia,* and also for determination of the species now named by him *Iphidea capensis* as being previously undescribed; and I have also to offer my thanks to Mr. F. P. Pascoe for kindly assisting identification of Longicorn beetles by lending specimens from his collection for comparison, and to Mr. W. L. Distant for identification of *Ptyelus grossus:* and likewise to Prof. Westwood, for examining and identifying for me the *Trilocha ficicola,* and also the specimen of *Ceratitis citriperda* figured at page 50, with its halberd-shaped head processes.

Most of the specimens and observations were forwarded to me through the hands of Mr. S. D. Bairstow, the originator of the work, who took great trouble in procuring information, and who also furnished valuable observations of his own, especially on the life-history of the *Icerya purchasi* or "Australian Bug," and its parasites, one of which — the *Coccinella* or Ladybird Beetle, the *Rodolia iceryæ* (see page 91)—has now, consequently on Mr. Bairstow's observations, been transmitted to New Zealand to prey on the *Iceryæ* of that island.

A special (though unhappily for her friends a posthumous) note of acknowledgment is owing to the late able and highly-gifted Lady Curator of the Albany Museum at Grahamstown,—Miss Glanville,—who for years had devoted special attention to the study of the habits of the crop pests of East Province, South Africa, and laid a foundation which it may be hoped will be of solid future benefit, and some of my best specimens were lent from the collection under her charge. Her communications to myself were marked by the same spirit of kindness and thoughtfulness which gained her the high esteem of her circle of South African friends; and though I have not been able to *show* her that at least some amount of progress has through her help been made in the work, she had so much at heart, I can at least offer my tribute of very sincere respect to the memory of a sister-worker.

This little book is offered in the hope that though it is but a fragment, yet still that, by descriptions and figures of even a few of the common farm insect-pests of the eastern parts of Cape Colony, it may possibly be of some agricultural service.

ELEANOR A. ORMEROD.

TORRINGTON HOUSE, ST. ALBAN'S, ENGLAND,
   May, 1889.

NOTES AND DESCRIPTIONS

OF A FEW

INJURIOUS FARM AND FRUIT INSECTS

OF

SOUTH AFRICA.

───────✦───────

ORDER COLEOPTERA.

FAM. MELOLONTHIDÆ.

ERIESTHIS STIGMATICA, Billb. (Fig. 1).

Trichius stigmaticus, Billb. Schönh. Syn. Ins. i. 3, App.
p. 44.
Eriesthis stigmatica, Burm. Handb. d. Entom. iv. 1, p. 51.

FIG. 1.—*Eriesthis stigmatica*, natural size and magnified.

Mealie Chafer : injurious to Mealies (Maize or Indian Corn).

Short-ovate ; head, thorax, under side, and legs black,
and densely clothed with fine grey pubescence ; base of
the thorax, the scutellum and elytra closely covered with
fine ochreous-yellow scales ; propygidium, pygidium, and
abdomen entirely covered with white scales, and variegated with brownish yellow markings ; each of the elytra
with five small black spots arranged in two oblique rows
of two and three each respectively, and several ill-defined

B

brownish longitudinal lines. The head is narrowed in front, with the margins slightly reflexed. The thorax is very convex, a little broader than long, narrowed in front and strongly rounded at the base; the entire surface is very closely punctured, and there is a slightly impressed longitudinal line in the centre. The scutellum is elongate and triangular. The elytra are together one-fourth broader than long, and strongly rounded at the sides; on the darker lines and spots there are short erect setæ, and similar setæ on the propygidium, pygidium, and sides of the abdomen. The legs are thick, especially the posterior ones; the anterior tibiæ have three large acute teeth (including the apical one), and the intermediate tibiæ a row of very small teeth on the external edge. The length of the body is 8—10 millm.

This species belongs to the sub-family *Hoplides*, and is allied to the common British *Hoplia philanthus*. In some specimens, probably owing to abrasion, the markings are less distinct and the colour altogether more obscure.—O. E. J.

Miss Glanville notes of this beetle that it destroys Mealie crops from near Fort Beaufort, right down to the Fish River mouth. Mr. Bairstow mentions that it appears to be the worst pest in the country for Mealies.

HYPOPHOLIS SOMMERI, Burm.   (Fig. 2).

H. sommeri, Burm. Handb. d. Entom. iv. 2, p. 283.
H. sulcicollis, Bohm. Ins. Caff. ii. p. 92.

FIG. 2.—*Hypopholis sommeri.*

Chafer injurious to Vines.

Ovate, convex; red-brown, shining; the elytra

luteous yellow, with a more or less clearly-defined red-brown band close to the lateral margin; the pygidium, under side, and legs with fine short depressed grey hairs. The head is broad, coarsely punctured, and has a fine impressed, slightly curved, transverse line in front; the clypeus is short and broadly rounded, with the margin a little reflexed, and the punctuation very coarse and confluent. The thorax is more than twice as broad at the base than long, it is rounded and narrowed at the sides in front, with the anterior angles considerably produced, the lateral margins are dilated and slightly reflexed, the entire surface is coarsely punctured, the punctures becoming closer and confluent towards the sides, and there is an impressed longitudinal line in the centre. The scutellum is rounded behind and of a nearly semicircular form, with a few coarse punctures. The elytra are broadest behind the middle, coarsely punctured, and have two slight elevated longitudinal lines on the disk. The pygidium is very closely and unevenly punctured. The under side is closely punctured, with the metasternum more sparsely punctured and longitudinally impressed in the centre; the mesosternal process is long and conical; in the male there is a longitudinal impression in the centre of the abdomen. The legs are moderately long and punctured, the anterior tibiæ are produced at the apex, and have a strong sub-apical tooth, and in the female there is an additional smaller tooth above this. The length of the body is 18—20 millm.

Judging by the number of specimens usually contained in collections received from S. Africa, this would appear to be a very common species in that country; it belongs to the sub-family *Melolonthides*, and is allied to the well-known *Melolontha vulgaris*, the "Cockchafer" of England.—O. E. J.

Miss Glanville sends this beetle for identification as a "pest from Vines," but gives no particulars as to habits or mode of attack.

Fig. 3 (p. 4) shows the appearance of the grub of the British Cockchafer, which, as a type of the larval form of the family of *Melolonths*, may be presumably taken as showing the form of the grubs of the Vine Cockchafer of S. Africa, the *H. sommeri*, mentioned above, and the preceding species.

FIG. 3.—British Cockchafer, grub and chrysalis.

The habits of various kinds of the so-called Cockchafers, or *Melolonths*, are for the beetles to feed on leafage, or vegetable matter above ground, and the grubs to feed under-ground, on roots of plants, grass, &c.

Where the beetles are sluggish during the day, and rest under the leafage of trees until they fly abroad in the twilight, much may be done to reduce the number by shaking them down. Pigs will eat them greedily, so will poultry; if there are more than can be got rid of by these means, the services of some boys to trample or beat the beetles by day would probably do all that is needed in the matter of destroying what may be knocked down at little cost.

With regard to destruction of the grubs, no plan seems (as far as I can find) to be known either in Europe, the E. Indies, or the U. S. A., for getting rid of them, excepting turning them out from under-ground and destroying them.

To give a single example of this, in Ceylon, where the grubs of various kinds of Chafers (*Melolonthidæ*) do much harm to Coffee-plant roots, it is noted by Mr. J. Nietner that on one estate, "A gang of Coolies was employed to dig them out of the ground (for they are always near the surface at the end of the feeding rootlets), which they did at the rate of about a quarter of a bushel per man per day. Still the Coffee recovered. .... Lime, salt, carbolic acid, and other remedies were tried, but without effect, I believe."*

As various kinds of Cockchafers feed at the roots of grasses, this fact might sometimes give a clue to where attack comes from, and when grass-land is being broken up,—or arable- or garden-land, known to be infested, is temporarily empty of crop,—hand-picking or turning on pigs, whilst the plough or spade are at work, would do good.

For prevention of injury from the above-mentioned and the preceding beetle-attack, specimens of the grubs are needed for figuring; likewise information as to what kinds of crops they chiefly feed at the roots of; how long they live; how deep they lie in the ground; how deep they go down to turn to the chrysalis condition; and also whether they are found at the roots of wild grasses or in decayed vegetable matter in woods. Also, what time of day or evening the beetles are in the quietest state, and what measures, if any, have been taken for reducing the numbers of the pest.

FAM. DYNASTIDÆ,

HETERONYCHUS ARATOR, Fab. (Fig. 4.)

Geotrupes arator, Fab. Ent. Syst. i. p. 88.
H. arator, Burm. Handb. d. Ent. v. p. 94; Bohm. Ins. Caff. ii. p. 9.

FIG. 4.—*Heteronychus arator.*

Very injurious generally, and especially to Wheat.

* 'The Coffee Tree and its Enemies.' By the late J. Nietner. Colombo. 1880.

Oblong, very convex, shining black, the under side, antennæ and legs piceous. The head is short and broad, closely rugulose, except at the base, where it is smooth; it has a fine transverse ridge in front, which curves inwardly on each side and joins the inner margin of the eyes; the margin of the clypeus is slightly reflexed and forms two obtuse points at the apex. The thorax is nearly twice as broad as long, with the sides and basal angles rounded and the anterior angles acute, the surface is without any punctuation, and there is a fine impressed marginal line at the sides and in front. The scutellum is broader than long, triangular, and smooth. The elytra have seven impressed longitudinal rows of punctures, the first, next the suture, is straight, the others are a little oblique; in some specimens the interstices have a few irregular punctures, and there is often an additional short row near the shoulder; the apex is coarsely punctured, and there is an impressed marginal line at the sides. The pygidium is very convex and smooth. The under surface has sparse brown hairs, and is punctured at the sides; the metasternum has a longitudinal impression in the centre. The legs are thick, with the tarsi slender, the anterior tibiæ have two strong teeth on the outer side, and the apex, rather obtuse, the middle and hinder tibiæ have two transverse ridges, which, as well as the apex, are spinose. The length of the body is 12—15 millm.

In general appearance this species somewhat resembles our common *Aphodius fossor*, but is rather larger; it belongs, however, to a quite distinct family, of which no member occurs in Britain.—O. E. J.

Miss Glanville's notes referring to this beetle state that it is the most wide-spread and destructive of the pests forwarded, and that it is a subterraneous worker, attacking the wheat by eating away the roots. It is said that it never attacks grain sown in ground newly broken up, even though it be within a yard of their old scene of operations. The ground must have been cultivated two or three years before they attack the crops on it. Even in the same field they sometimes leave large patches unmolested. It also destroys potatoes, eating them out and leaving only the empty skin. The remedy proposed by Dr. Becker and the Rev. N. Abraham consists of traps of manure placed at intervals throughout the fields, in which heaps the beetles will doubtless lay their eggs. When the grubs are hatched the heaps may be carted away to the fowl-yard, where they will be speedily put an end to.

Farmers complain, however, that these beetles are found on lands that have never been manured, and therefore conclude that the above remedy is useless. One farmer put lime on his field, and reports that it has killed the beetles.

Mr. Bairstow mentions that numerous reports are to hand of the destructiveness of this beetle, which, either in the larval or perfect stage, creates great havoc amongst crops; also that he has observed it in thousands on a hot night at Emerald Hill.

The following observations, contributed by Mr. Fred. R. Schauble, of Stortge, refer to this pest under the local name of "Keever-beetle":—

"These insects have for the last three or four years been very destructive in our crops. The beetle goes by the name of 'Keever' amongst the farmers, and I have no doubt is well known. . . . . They are rarely seen above-ground, and bite off the crops about an inch under-ground. Last year they were very partial and particularly destructive, in some cases destroying as many as fifteen to twenty acres of growing wheat. As a rule, they are principally found in red ground. . . . . Just now they are doing a great deal of damage; some of my neighbours say that we are generally troubled by them in dry seasons. They feed on the crops from the time they are grown three or four inches above the ground.

"My object in writing to you and sending the sample of beetle is to see if you can perhaps advise me how to destroy them—whether anything can be applied to the soil while ploughing. I was advised to sprinkle with salt. This has been tried by a man living in Nanaga, but has not succeeded. They appear in great numbers. Nov. 3, 1885."

This beetle is found throughout Caffraria ('Insecta Caffrariæ,' Part II., p. 9).

Of this beetle, namely, the *Heteronychus arator*, Burm., it is noted by Mr. T. Vernon Wollaston that it is found in St. Helena, "and it has much the appearance of being truly indigenous, though found equally in Southern Africa. It occurs at intermediate and rather lofty altitudes, its normal range being from about 2000 to 3000 ft. above the sea." .... "It is more particularly along the sides of the roads that it is practically to be met with, 'in the neighbourhood,' as Mr. Melliss well observes, ' of grass-lands and hay-fields,' where it may often be seen lying dead in considerable numbers, or crawling sluggishly about amongst the loose, friable, dusty soil."* ...

The above notes point to this "Keever Beetle" being a grass as well as corn-pest, and may give some clue as to where to look for the grubs, as in common course of things beetles die just after having laid their eggs. Judging by the observations respectively of Mr. Bairstow and Miss Glanville, it is the habit of these beetles, when in what may be called active life, to fly about trees on hot nights, and to go down a little below the surface of the ground during the day.

The appearance of the grub is not mentioned, but it may be presumed not to vary from the others of the family of the *Dynastidæ*, to which it belongs, in any important point, and it might be expected to be a long, thick, whitish, fleshy grub, generally resembling those figured at pp. 4 and 13, but of a much smaller size. The three pairs of stout legs, the definite head furnished with jaws, and the habit of lying on one side when in repose, are some of the points by which the grubs

---

* 'Coleoptera Sancta Helenæ,' p. 64.

of this Lamellicorn Division may usually be known at a glance.

During some correspondence with coffee-planters in Ceylon relatively to prevention of Chafer-attack, I was informed that the nature of the soil (as mentioned above with regard to the S. African Corn Chafer) made a great deal of difference in the amount of attack, and the custom of filling little pits with manure to act as traps was also mentioned.

Looking at the point that the beetles appear to go down or creep in the surface by day, and come up at night, it would seem that some dressing, such as paraffin and sand, or ashes or dry earth, might be worth trying. A mixture of a quart of paraffin to a bushel of the dry material has been found not to do the slightest harm to tender Hop-shoots sprouting through it, and to prevent Aphides coming up. The smell might be expected to be a great preventive of attack.

Information is needed as to where the grubs live, whether they are found at the roots of the corn or in manure or decayed vegetable-matter, and specimens also are needed.

Any information as to whether beetle-attack is worst near woods would be useful, and any notes of experiments which may have been tried of result of application of chemical manures, such as lime, gas-lime, nitrate of soda, sulphate of potash, or sulphate of ammonia, in case these are procurable.

The same kind of information is also much needed regarding the two following " Corn Chafer " attacks, namely, those of the *Pentodon nircus* and *P. contractus*, and it may be remarked in passing, that it would be an immense help to all concerned to have information as to what generally intelligible name might be adopted for the crop-pests, such as has been given in the case of the " Keever Beetle."

PENTODON NIREUS, Burm. (Fig. 5).

Pentodon nireus, Burm. Handb. d. Entom. v. p. 103 ; Bohm. Ins. Caff. ii. p. 8.

FIG. 5.—1, *Pentodon nireus* ; 2, *P. contractus.*

This Species and the next are Wheat-pests.

Short-ovate, very convex; black, above slightly shining, under side and legs piceous, shining; club of the antennæ red-brown. The head is short and broad, with close, confluent, coarse punctures, and a fine elevated transverse line in front; the clypeus has two small raised points at the apex. The thorax is broader than long, with the sides rounded behind and narrowed in front, the anterior angles are produced and acute, the entire surface is evenly and rather closely punctured, and the anterior and lateral margins are slightly reflexed. The scutellum is broader than long, slightly impressed in the centre, and without punctures. The elytra are together, in the middle, nearly as broad as long, rounded at the sides, and very convex; there is a straight impressed row of punctures next the suture and six to eight slightly oblique rows on the disk, the inner rows are distinct, but the outer ones are more or less effaced, especially towards the apex, in some specimens. The pygidium is short, convex, and punctured. The under side and legs are punctured and sparsely clothed with long red-brown hairs, the centre of the metasternum and abdomen are smooth, the former having a broad median impression, the legs are thick, the anterior tibiæ have two very stout teeth on the outer edge and one at the apex, the intermediate and posterior tibiæ have the apical margin and two transverse ridges on the outer side armed with small spines. The length of the body is 15—18 millm.— O. E. J.

Found throughout Caffraria ('Insecta Caffrariæ.').

PENTODON CONTRACTUS, Bohm. (Fig. 5).

Pentodon contractus, Bohm. Ins. Caff. ii. p. 4.

This species is very similar to the preceding, but is of a rather smaller size and of a duller black above, the head is less closely punctured in the middle and smooth at the base and apex, with the transverse line almost obsolete, and the apical margin of the clypeus more strongly reflexed and without points, the basal margin of the thorax is straighter, the scutellum is smaller, and the elytra are shorter and more rounded, with the rows of punctures more regular, and the interstices slightly convex. The length of the body is 12—14 millm.

Both the foregoing species of *Pentodon* have been forwarded as Wheat-pests, which are believed to be similar in their mode of attack to the *Heteronychus arator*. As the two genera are closely allied, their habits are probably similar. Both the species of *Pentodon* are to be easily distinguished from *H. arator* by their larger, more ovate and convex form and duller colour.—O. E. J.

Occurs in the region of the River Limpopo ('Insecta Caffrariæ.').

FAM. CETONIIDÆ.

RHABDOTIS SEMIPUNCTATA, Fab. (Fig. 6).

Cetonia semipunctata, Fab. Ent. Syst. i. 2, p. 140.
C. chalca, Gory et Perch. Mon. Cet. p. 285, t. 44, f. 5.
Rhabdotis chalcea, Burm. Handb. d. Entom. iii. p. 528.

Ovate and moderately convex; bright green; a line on each side of the head and four slightly curved longitudinal lines on the thorax, white; each of the elytra with two lines on the basal half and eight or nine spots on the apical half, white; pygidium white, with a central longitudinal green line; beneath white, and with sparse

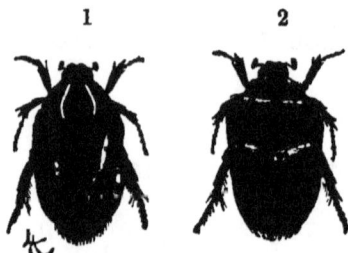

FIG. 6.—*Rhabdotis semipunctata.* 1, upper side; 2, under side.

Injurious to Figs and Peaches, and earlier in the season to the blossoms of Apples and Plums.

brownish-grey hairs at the sides, shining green in the centre, the apical segment of the abdomen and a small spot on each side of the other segments also green; the legs are green and fringed on the inner side with brownish-grey hairs, a broad stripe on the under side of the femora, a small spot on the knees, and a short stripe at the base of the tibiæ, white. The head is nearly flat and closely punctured, with the clypeus a little rounded at the sides and slightly emarginate at the apex. The thorax is very sparingly punctured, with the sides rounded and the base trisinuous. The scutellum is large, triangular, and sparsely punctured. The elytra are punctured in rows and rugulose at the apex, the suture is a little raised and slightly produced at the apical angle. The under side is smooth in the centre. The male has a slightly impressed central line on the abdomen, and the anterior tibiæ narrow and without teeth on the outer edge; in the female the abdomen is more convex, punctured at the apex and without a central

line, and the anterior tibiæ have an acute tooth near the
the apex. The length of the body is 17—19 millm.

This very pretty beetle is allied to *Cetonia aurata*, the
common "Rose Chafer" of England; it may be readily
recognised by its bright green upper surface, and the
clearly-defined white lines and spots.—O. E. J.

Mr. E. de Witt Meulen, of the Winterhoek, Uitenhage,
reports that this species is common in his part of the
country, appearing about October on Fig and Peach
trees just when the fruits are beginning to ripen, and
devouring them before they have time to mature. The
only fruits saved were those enclosed in small bags tied
round them. Mr. Bairstow remarks that it is rather
scarce in his district, appears much earlier, and attacks
the Apple and Plum blossoms.

Fig. 7.—Grub of English Rose Chafer.

The grubs of the *Cetoniidæ* feed on roots of plants,
and are also found in rotten vegetable-matter, decayed
wood, dung, &c.

The above figure of the grub of the common "Rose
Chafer" of England, the *Cetonia aurata*, gives a general
idea of the appearance of the grubs of this family,
which of course vary, like the beetles, much in size.

In Canada a kind known as the "Indian *Cetonia*"
does much mischief by eating into Pears, Peaches, and
Grapes; and a nearly allied kind is known in more
southern parts as the "Fig-eater," but it is noted by
Professor Saunders, in his excellent work on 'Insects
injurious to Fruits' of N. America, that as yet, no
remedy has been found for this trouble excepting
catching the insects and destroying them.

If the S. African Cetonias fly in the bright sunshine, their numbers (in garden treatment, at least) might be reduced as they are in England by catching them with nets on poles ; but otherwise the only methods of prevention appear to be those previously mentioned for the corn or·plant chafers.

Fᴀᴍ. ANOBIIDÆ.

Aɴᴏʙɪᴜᴍ ᴘᴀɴɪᴄᴇᴜᴍ, Linn.

Dermestes paniceus, Linn. Fauna Suec. p. 145.
Anobium minutum, Fab. Ent. Syst. i. p. 238.

Fɪɢ. 8.—Piece of a boot injured by maggot of *Anobium paniceum.*

Paste Beetle ; " Boot Beetle."

Oblong, convex; reddish brown, and closely covered with very fine short grey pubescence. The head is deflexed and concealed beneath the front margin of the thorax; the antennæ have the basal joint rather large, the second smaller, the six following very small, and the apical three very large and rather more than twice as long as broad. The thorax is very convex and finely punctured, a little wider than the elytra at the base, rounded at the sides, somewhat compressed in front, and slightly impressed on each side at the base. The scutellum is small and nearly square. The elytra are straight at the sides, rounded behind, and have ten impressed rows of fine punctures on each ; there is also a short and slightly oblique row of similar punctures on either side of the scutellum, the interstices between the rows of punctures are flat, and have indistinct transverse scratches. In fresh and perfect specimens the pubescence is very close, and imparts a dusty appearance to the surface ; there are also some longer hairs between the rows of punctures on the elytra, but in old and worn specimens the surface is frequently more or less denuded of hairs, and has a much more polished appearance. The length of the body is from 3 to $3\frac{1}{2}$ millm.—O. E. J.

This destructive little beetle is closely allied to the common English "Death Watch" (*Anobium domesticum*), which is well known from the injury it occasions by its borings in furniture and the wooden fittings of houses. It is very common in Europe and many other parts of the world, and has been found feeding on various substances, such as ginger, rhubarb, Cayenne pepper, wafers, ship-biscuit, &c., and it is recorded that, in the larva state, it has been known to perforate tinfoil.

In the course of 1885 and 1886 I received various communications from manufacturers and exporters in England, and also from recipients of the goods at Port Elizabeth, Cape. Colony, S. Africa, regarding injury caused to exported boots by insect-workings. A pair of children's boots, which were sent to me, as a sample of the attack, irom an English manufacturer, were so exceedingly injured by the small galleries run by maggots in the parts where paste had been used (in making the boots) to fasten the linings and leather together, that the leather was partly perforated and was literally in rags at the upper part, and the boots consequently were totally useless.

Figure 8 (page 14) shows the appearance of the

maggot-galleries, which were for the most part where the paste had been applied, but in some places ran further on, and were as clearly traceable as those of many kinds of maggots often are between the bark and wood of attacked trees.

At first there was some uncertainty as to the kind of beetle that caused the damage, but on the samples of injured boots being sent, I found the beetle was present in the galleries, as well as the dead maggot, and that it was the well-known and destructive *Anobium paniceum*, the so-called "Paste Beetle" of Europe.

The method of life of the *Anobium paniceum* in the attack under consideration was obviously for the maggots to feed in the infested boot between the linen and leather (as described above), and there to turn to chrysalids, from which in due time the beetles came out. We found the insect present in all its stages,—larva, pupa, and perfect beetle,—in the injured manufactures.

The maggots were too much dried to allow of precise description of their appearance in life, but this special kind is described by Prof. Westwood as being white and curved, and similar to those of other *Anobia*. These resemble Chafer maggots in miniature, being soft, cylindrical, fleshy, and slightly pilose, with a scaly head (armed with robust-toothed jaws); six legs; the last segment of the body large.*

At what stage of the making of the boots, or of their exportation, or of their storage on arrival at the Colony, the attack commenced there was no evidence given. It was stated by one of the firms in correspondence with me, that they did not find the attack in goods which remained in their retail shops in England even for two or three years, and also that they never had complaints regarding infestation of goods exported to Australia or to the Brazils, but nearly all the complaints came from Cape Town, or from Port Elizabeth, in Cape Colony.

---

* The above description of *Anobium* larvæ is abridged from that given in Prof. Westwood's 'Introd. to Classification of Insects,' vol. i. p. 271.

How the attack was set on foot remained unknown, but the damage caused was very serious. Mr. Bairstow communicated on this subject as follows : " This beetle has proved most disastrous to the boot and shoe trade in Port Elizabeth " ; and, relatively to means of prevention, reported observations to the effect that socks containing alum were free from insect-attack. In confirmation of this socks were shown, one of which that had been dipped in alum being free from attack, and the other, which had not been dipped, being infested. This agrees with observations as far back as the time of Linnæus, that these grubs would be destroyed by alum.

With regard to preventive measures which might be serviceably applied in the process of making the boots, it appeared that as the attack was limited, or almost entirely limited, to the parts where paste had been used in manufacture, that the thing needed was either the mixture of some chemical with the paste which, though poisonous to the maggot, would be harmless to the boot-makers and likewise non-injurious to the boots ; or, if it could be done without causing difficulty in working the needles, to use paste with the nutritious part of the flour removed, and thus, even if the beetle-eggs were laid, any maggots hatching from them would die for want of food.

In the practical working of these plans there were, however, some difficulties. These matters I went into at the time with some of our chief manufacturing or exporting firms, and also, through the courtesy of Prof. Bernard Dyer, of Great Tower Street, London, was favoured with analyses of the materials used for the above purpose, namely, for forming in-nutritious paste, of which samples were sent me for investigation.

As widespread business interests are involved in the considerations of the details of this attack, its causes and its cure, I have not thought it desirable to go in full here into these points ; but I preserve the letters for reference in case of need, and, if desired for practical use, would gladly give any information in my power to any applicant personally interested.

C

FAM. TENEBRIONIDÆ.

PSAMMODES OBLIQUATUS, Sol. (Fig. 9.)

Psammodes obliquatus, Solier, Mem. Ac. Torin. 1844, p. 309.

FIG. 9.—*Psammodes obliquatus.*

Injurious to Mealies.

Elongate-ovate, convex, piceous-black or red-brown; head, thorax, and under side dull, the elytra shining. The head is flat and finely punctured, with the eyes small and prominent; the front part is a little convex, more sparingly punctured and shining; the antennæ are dull brown, sparsely pubescent, with the base and apex reddish. The thorax is transverse, broadest in the middle, with the basal and anterior angles a little produced and rounded, convex in the centre, and closely covered with fine setiferous punctures; the sides are a little reflexed and transversely wrinkled. The scutellum is very closely punctured, short and almost entirely concealed when the thorax is raised. The elytra have three slightly oblique longitudinal ridges on each, which do not extend quite to the apex; these ridges and the elevated sutural margin are closely punctured and covered with coarse depressed brownish setæ; the other parts have coarser remote punctures furnished with similar setæ, the outer margin is reflexed, and the apex has a small notch at the suture. The under side and legs are black or piceous, and closely covered with fine setiferous punctures; the tarsi are reddish. The length of the body is 14—15 millm.

This beetle is usually found covered with a coating of mud, which the rough setiferous surface renders very difficult to remove; in its earthy clothing it would scarcely be recognized from the above description, as the colour and punctation is entirely hidden.

The genus *Psammodes* belongs to the subfamily *Molurides*, and is confined to Africa; very little appears to be known of their habits, although several species are very common at the Cape. The general aspect of many of the species is not unlike some of the *Carabidæ*, but in having only four joints to the posterior tarsi (hinder pair of feet) they may be readily distinguished from that family, in which all the tarsi are five-jointed.—O. E. J.

Miss Glanville has sent this beetle for identification, as "a Mealie pest received from Albany in 1885."

OPATRUM MICANS, Germ. (Fig. 10.)

Opatrum micans, Germar, Ins. Spec. Nov. p. 145.

FIG. 10.—*Opatrum micans*, magnified and nat. size.

Injurious to Carrot-roots and Potato-leafage.

Elongate-ovate, somewhat depressed, dull brownish black, and closely covered with short depressed brownish grey hairs. The head is short, broad, flat and closely covered with confluent punctures; there is a slight, curved, transverse impression in front of the eyes, and the front of the clypeus has a deep central notch; the antennæ are nearly twice as long as the head, and gradually thickened towards the apex; the seven basal

joints are shining red-brown, the others are dull piceous.
The thorax is as broad as the elytra at the base, the
sides are rounded and narrowed to the front, with the
anterior angles produced on each side of the head to the
front of the eyes; the punctation is very close and
confluent, and there is a slight longitudinal line in the
centre. The scutellum is nearly semicircular, a little
broader than long, slightly punctured and shining. The
elytra are nearly straight at the sides, slightly broader
in the middle, and have nine impressed rows of large
deep punctures on each, the interstices are slightly
convex and finely punctured. The under side and legs
are rather closely punctured, shining, and with the
pubescence more sparse than on the upper side; the
tibiæ towards the apex and the tarsi are red-brown or
piceous. The length of the body is 8—9 millm.

The genus *Opatrum* belongs to the *Opatrides*, a distinct
subfamily from the preceding; nearly 150 species are
now known from various parts of the Old World; they
are usually found in sandy and barren districts, and
often occur in great profusion. The only species found
in England (*O. sabulosum*) is very common on the coast
in sandy and muddy localities.—O. E. J.

This beetle is reported by Miss Glanville to destroy
carrots in much the same way as *Heteronychus arator*
does the potatoes, also that it has been observed feeding
on the leaves of potato.

It is noted of the *Opatrum hadroides*, Woll., the species
widely distributed in St. Helena, that it occurs beneath
stones, likewise that "Mr. Melliss mentions that he has
frequently observed it in great profusion on ploughed
fields at Longwood and in potato-grounds,"* which last
observation of locality agrees with the observation of
Miss Glanville regarding that of the above species, the
O. micans.

* 'Coleoptera Sancta Helenæ,' by T. Vernon Wollaston, p. 225.

FAM. CANTHARIDÆ.

MYLABRIS OCULATA, Thunb. (Fig. 11.)
MYLABRIS LUNATA, Pall. (Fig. 12.)

FIG. 11.—*Mylabris oculata.*

Injurious to Peas and Beans, likewise hurtful to fruit-blossom.

Of this family, to which the well-known Blister
Beetle or Spanish Fly (*Cantharis vesicatoria*), belongs,
Miss Glanville has submitted seven species for determination; these prove to be as follows:—*Mylabris
oculata*, Thunbg., *M. 16-guttata*, Thunbg., *M. capensis*,
Linn., *M. groendali*, Billbg., *M. lunata*, Pall., *M. undata*,
Thunbg., and *Lytta pallidipennis*, Haag. The last-
mentioned species is one of the true *Cantharidæ*; the
others have been separated by some authors as a distinct
family under the name of *Mylabridæ*, the principal dis-
tinction being that the antennæ are long and filiform in
the former and shorter and conspicuously thickened
towards the apex in the latter. The *Mylabridæ* possess
the same vesicating properties as the true *Cantharidæ*,
and are very similar to them in form; the majority of
the species are black with yellow or red bands and
markings on the elytra, and it is the shape and extent
of these markings which is chiefly used to distinguish
the species. Many species of this family are found in
South Africa, and as Mr. Bairstow remarks that "all
our *Mylabridæ* are scourges," it would be of little service
to give a detailed description of the species sent.

M. oculata, of which a figure is given above, is one of
the largest and most conspicuous species of the genus ;
the body and legs are black and rather shining, with
short black hairs ; the antennæ are yellow, and there is
a small round spot at the base of each of the elytra, and
two broad bands extending right across them of a dark
amber-yellow.   Mr. Bairstow notes the injurious nature
of " all our *Mylabridæ*," and also that he had observed
this species on the blossoms of fruit trees.

Fig. 12.—*Mylabris lunata*.

M. lunata, of which a figure is also given, is about
half the size of *M. oculata*, and has the yellow bands on
the elytra much narrower, and the round basal spot
which is present in that species, is here replaced by a
curved yellow mark or lunule.   This species is stated
by Mr. Bairstow to be very common in the district of
Albany, Peddie, and Fish River, destroying peas and
beans.

FAM. BRUCHIDÆ.

BRUCHUS sp. — ? (SUBARMATUS, Gyll. ?).   (Fig. 13.)

The South African Bean-seed Beetle does not quite
agree with any species of which descriptions have been
published ; it approaches very close to the *B. subarmatus*,
Gyll., and may eventually prove to be that species, but
as the specimens forwarded for determination are not in
good condition the question of specific identity is left
open for the present.   About 400 species of this genus
have now been described from various parts of the world,
and as they, from their habits, are peculiarly liable to
transmission from one country to another it renders the
determination of a species often a very tedious matter,

and especially difficult when the specimens are imperfect
and abraded.

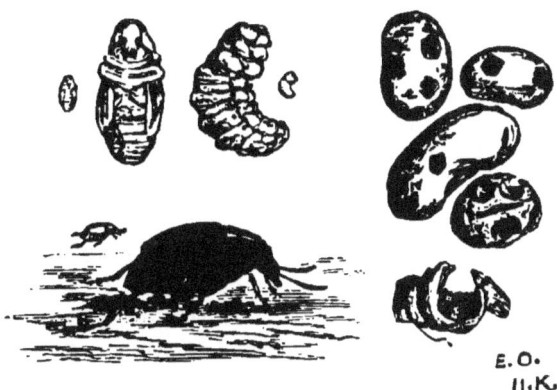

Fig. 13.—*Bruchus subarmatus*, Gyll.?

Beetle, maggot, and chrysalis, all natural size and magnified; injured
beans; and fragment of case of chrysalis magnified.

The above figures are taken from the specimens forwarded by Mr. Bairstow from Port Elizabeth, including
the three stages of larva, pupa, and imago, together
with injured beans, which in some instances still contained the pupa or imago. A description of the perfect
beetle is as follows :—

The upper surface is black, slightly shining, and with
fine depressed ashy brown pubescence. The head is very
finely punctured, with the eyes large and prominent,
and the forehead convex; the antennæ are black, with
the four basal joints dull red. The thorax is closely
punctured, a little rounded at the sides and obliquely
narrowed in front, the base is a little produced in the
middle over the scutellum, and has a slight central
impression and notch, the pubescence is closer and
forms a pale narrow longitudinal line in the centre.
The scutellum is nearly square, with a small central
notch behind. The elytra are very finely and closely
punctured with ten impressed rows of larger punctures
on each; there are three indistinct transverse marks

produced by a paucity or absence of the pubescence.
The under side is black or piceous, very finely punctured, and has a similar pubescence to the upper side;
the sides and the apex of the abdomen and the pygidium
are dull red. The legs are entirely dull red, with the
exception of the posterior femora, which are black on
the under side, and have a small acute tooth near the
apex. The length of the body is 4 millm.

Of the British *Bruchi* this species is most nearly
allied to *B. loti*. Compared with our well-known Bean-
seed Beetle (*B. rufimanus*, Boh.), it is smaller, rather
more depressed above, has a narrower thorax, without
teeth at the sides, and has the posterior femora furnished
with a small acute tooth near the apex; the colour of
the middle and hind legs, and the markings on the elytra
are also different.—O. E. J.

Judging both from the specimens and the descriptions forwarded, the attack of this Seed-weevil is
seriously hurtful. In two of the beans figured above
I found four holes showing where beetles had escaped,
in another seven beetles had been present, and in
another I found five beetles or coloured chrysalids still
within. Mr. S. D. Bairstow reported that "This pest,
when in larval condition, reduces the interior of the
seed to a fine powder, and passes into pupa sometimes in
its powdery bed, which disappears almost immediately
on the emergence of the perfect insect." Mr. Bairstow
also mentions that the kind of bean which these Seed-
weevils most attack is the Sugar-bean (a white one),
but that many varieties of beans are grown which they
attack also.

The common method of proceeding of *Bruchi*—that
is, of Pea- or Bean-seed Weevils—is for the female
beetle to lay her eggs on the young pod or seed-vessel
whilst still in its early state in the flower. From these
eggs the maggots hatch and eat their way into the
seeds—it may be one maggot or it may be several to
each seed—and within this seed they usually feed till

the time comes for them to turn to chrysalids, and thence to beetles. In the case of the common Broadbean *Bruchus* of England, the maggot gnaws a tunnel to the outside of the bean, but does not gnaw a road through the outer skin, so that the small round film of skin remains as a covering to the gallery, and when the time comes for the beetle to escape it just presses off the lid, as it may be called, and creeps out. According to circumstances, it may come out in heaps of granaried seed, or in seed sown in the field, and in due season it flies to the blossoms of the beans or peas, or other plants, wild or cultivated, of bean or pea kind suitable for the food of the maggots, and there it starts a new attack.

The infested beans, and also the maggots, forwarded from Port Elizabeth, show a slight difference respectively in method of attack, and in structure, to what has usually been recorded. Instead of the maggot-tunnels ending as soon as they came to the outside of the bean, I found that they sometimes ran on just under the skin, so that their shape and the blackish colour of the insects when developed to the beetle state could be distinctly seen through the thin transparent coat of the bean. Also in some instances it appeared from the gnawings that the maggot had made, or might have made, its entrance into the seed *from the outside*. This point should be ascertained by examination of pods on the plant; but so far as can be judged from the shape of the cavities, and from the appearance of the opening outside the bean, it appeared to have been entered as above mentioned.

The habit of straying from one seed to another, when the first locality is unsatisfactory, has been recorded in the case of the Lentil Bruchus (*B. lentis*) from careful observations by Heeger.*

It appears from these that, when the original quarters no longer suit them, the maggots wander away at evening to seek another dwelling; in still weather, it is stated, "they let themselves fall to the ground, and

---

* 'Praktische Insekten Kunde,' by Dr. E. L. Taschenberg, pt. ii. p. 267.

by the help of their strong jaws writhe themselves along until they find a pod hanging down conveniently for them, into which they eat without delay."

In the case of the S. African Bean-seed Maggot, the view of it being able to travel about inside the pod,—whatever it may do outside,—is confirmed by the structure of the maggot. On microscopic examination, I found that it was, as is usual in other species of *Bruchi*, much corrugated, but also that the three segments next to the head were distinctly divided beneath from each other, and that each of these segments was furnished with a pair of appendages placed in the common position of feet, and, as far as I could see, answering the purpose of the three pairs of claw-feet which are to be found in many beetle-grubs.

In the description of the maggot of the Pea Bruchus (*B. pisi*, Linn.), given by John Curtis, in his 'Farm Insects' (p. 359), he mentions that the maggots are legless, or have very minute feet; this would exactly suit the state of affairs with the S. African maggot. The appendages appeared one-jointed, and slightly conical, or curved. It has not been generally observed that the maggot forms a cell of the destroyed matter round it in which to turn to chrysalis. In some instances this was so strong that the substance of the bean might be broken away from it, as is shown by the magnified figure of a small broken piece of the cell. In the infested English beans this chrysalis-case may be easily observed by soaking the bean for a few hours in water. It then loosens from the gallery and adheres closely to the beetle within it, and in cases of steeps being used to destroy the pest, this adherence of the covering sodden with poisonous matter to the insect would be of practical service.

Means of Prevention and Remedy.

Where beans are to be sown immediately, and there is no likelihood of frost ensuing, steeps might be used with good effect to kill the beetles in infested beans.

I have found by experiment with English beans, that in four-and-twenty hours, or possibly rather more, the moisture would soak into the infested bean so as to destroy the beetle, which I found almost always dead, with the case or cocoon above mentioned clinging round it. I only used water, my object being merely to ascertain whether moisture would pass in; but in case of some of the regular seed-steeps being used, I should not consider they could fail of being of use.

It has been found by English experiment in the course of the present year that dressing seed with Calvert's Carbolic-acid answered; this, of course, diluted to a strength enough to kill the insects without damaging the seed. For a good working recipe for this purpose I am obliged to Mr. George Street, of Maulden, Ampt-hill, Bedfordshire. He used a mixture of one pint of M'Dougall's " Sewage Carbolic," 1 ℔. of blue vitriol and six quarts of water to six bushels of beans. This dressing was applied to the beans in the same way as that used for seed-wheat. The beans came up well, made good progress, and Mr. Street informed me, after waiting some time to be able to tell with certainty, that the result was thoroughly satisfactory.

The method of poisoning the seed by fumigation, which is used in Canada,—where the Pea-weevil is so exceedingly injurious that it requires to be carefully kept in check,—is very simple, and is stated to be of much use. This is by placing bisulphide of carbon in a large vessel with the infested seeds, which are thus brought under the influence of the poisonous vapour, and the beetles within are thus destroyed before they have the opportunity of flying away to commence new attack.

When once attack has begun on the seed in the pod, or rather on the pod, whilst it is still so young in the centre of the bean-blossoms that the seed is hardly to be seen within—then it is too late to apply any remedy; therefore it is highly needful to kill the pest in the seeds before they are sown, or so to manage that the beetles may be kept away as far as can be from the crop.

Before buying seed, a sample should be examined to see whether it is then, or has been, infested. If beetles are in it at the time this will be known by the creatures or their galleries showing through the slightly transparent skin of the bean, as I have observed in some instances of S. African bean-seed attack, or by a little round depression in the skin showing where the end of the gallery reaches the skin, as is the case in English attack. If beetles have been present, but are gone out of the seed, this will be known by the seed having little holes like shot-holes into it.

Seed which either is or has been much infested should not be used, because what has been eaten away by the maggots will so much lessen the seed-leaves which help to support the young plant in its first growth, that it will consequently be weaker, or possibly not shoot at all.

Sweeping up the beetles in seed-lofts, or the like places where beans may be stored, and destroying them, would, of course, be serviceable, and they should be looked for on the ceilings as well as elsewhere. The beetles live for several weeks at least in this state, for Mr. S. D. Bairstow notes with regard to this Bean-seed Weevil, " Some of the beetles watched by me have lived in the perfect state for five weeks, and are living at the time of writing."

Where any area, large or small, is much infested, a complete change of crop, so as to ensure absence of beans for two or three years, is highly desirable. If this can be carried out in a district by common consent,— and other leguminous plants, whether wild or cultivated, which this beetle attacks, kept under,—the absence of the proper food necessarily enormously lessens the amount of the feeders, and clears out the attack for a while.

The means of prevention may be stated shortly as :— destroying the beetle in the seed by steeping or by fumigating; destroying the beetles in seed-lofts, if they are noticeable ; carefully avoiding sowing infected seed ; and rotation of crops in infested districts.

Fam. LAMIIDÆ.

CEROPLESIS BICINCTA, Fab. (Fig. 14.)

Lamia bicincta, Fab. Ent. Syst. Suppl. p. 145.
L. caffra, Thunb. Mus. Nat. Ups. iv. p. 58, t. 1, f. 1.
Cerambyx continuus, Oliv. Ent. iv. 67, p. 123, t. 23, f. 7.
C. orientalis, Herbst, Füssl. Arch. vii. p. 168, t. 45, f. 10.
Ceroplesis thunbergii, Führs. Ofvers. Kongl. Ak. Forhl. 1872, 2, p. 41.
C. sumptuosa, Pasc. Ann. Mag. Nat. Hist. 4, xv. p. 66.

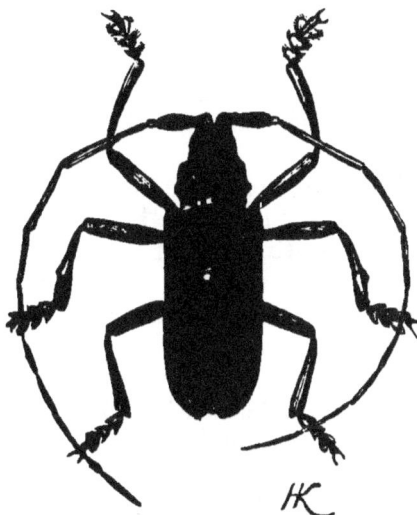

Fig 14.—*Ceroplesis bicincta.*

Willow Beetle.

Oblong, subcylindrical; dull black, with sparse short yellowish-grey hairs; thorax black or covered with a deep red or claret-coloured tomentum; elytra slightly metallic, or greenish black, with two narrow red bands dividing them transversely into three nearly equal parts; the apex generally with a marginal band or spot of the same colour. The head is coriaceous, flattened in front and slightly rugulose; the antennæ are each inserted in a large obtuse prominence between the eyes, and divided

by a deeply impressed central line; in the male the
antennæ are half as long again as the body, in the
female scarcely longer than the body. The thorax is
slightly impressed and constricted in front and behind,
coarsely rugose, and with an obtuse tubercle on each
side behind the middle. The scutellum is rounded
behind and impressed at the base and in the centre.
The elytra are very closely and irregularly punctured;
at the base the punctures are very coarse, deep, and
confluent, towards the apex they become smaller and
shallower, the shoulders are prominent and obtuse.
The under side and legs are coriaceous, and the tarsi
are very broad; in the male the anterior and middle
tibiæ are slightly curved, and the anterior tarsi are
fringed with long black hairs. The length of the body
is 20—35 millm.

This beautiful but common South African "Longhorn" varies very much in size, the bands on the elytra
vary a little in width, and in colour from pink to
vermilion: these varieties have been named and re-
named several times by different writers. In the typical
bicincta the apical marginal band of the elytra is absent;
in some specimens this is only represented by a small
spot, and in others it extends along the side margin and
joins the second transverse band. The figure is taken
from a large male example which, from a comparison
with the actual type, is found to agree precisely with
sumptuosa, and is also very similar to the variety
described and figured by Herbst under the name of
orientalis.

Ceroplesis thunbergii of the 'Coleoptera Caffrariæ' is
evidently described from small and very fresh specimens
of this species, in which the thorax, base of the elytra,
and the under side have a red tomentose clothing; this
tomentum is usually present on the thorax, but many
apparently worn specimens are quite destitute of it. In
these specimens the elytra generally have a more metallic
or greenish lustre.—O. E. J.

CEROPLESIS HOTTENTOTTA, Fab. (Fig. 15.)

Lamia hottentotta, Fab. Syst. Ent. p. 173 ; Oliv. Ent. iv.
67, p. 90, t. 4, f. 27.

Cerambyx lanius, Voet, Cat. ii. p. 13, t. 11, f. 45.

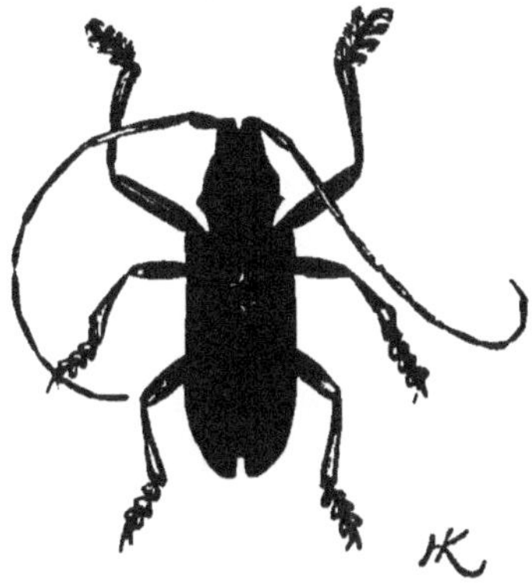

FIG. 15.—*Ceroplesis hottentotta.*

This species is very similar to *C. bicincta*, but is usually smaller, narrower, and of a duller colour, the red bands on the elytra are rather broader and less clearly defined, and the second one never extends more than half-way across each of the elytra, on the outer side, and is sometimes only represented by a small marginal spot. The tubercles in which the antennæ are inserted are less prominent and wider apart, and the thorax is more coarsely and sparsely punctured. As in the preceding species, the red tomentose clothing varies in different individuals; in some, apparently freshly-emerged specimens, it is present on the legs, as well as the head, thorax, base of the elytra, and under side. The length of the body is 17—23 millm.—O. E. J.

Mr. Bairstow, writing from Port Elizabeth, observed : —" The *Ceroplesis* is very injurious, and the great scourge of our Willows ; it is in hundreds up the garden-drive to Emerald Hill, on either side of which are

Willows.　It is, perhaps, the commonest 'Longhorn' throughout the province.　The larva burrows in the Willows much like *Prionus*."

Miss Glanville, writing from Grahamstown, also noted the *Ceroplesis* as destructive, whilst in larval condition, to fruit-trees, and that the perfect insect had been found dead beneath the bark, having been unable, from some accidental cause, to escape.

The above notes are appended, in the observations sent accompanying the insects, to the numbers applying to both the above species of *Ceroplesis*.

ALPHITOPOLA MACULOSA, Pasc.　(Fig. 16.)

Alphitopola maculosa, Pascoe, Trans. Ent. Soc. Lond. 2, iv. p. 251; Führs. Ofvers. Kongl. Ak. Forhl. 1872, 2, p. 32.

FIG. 16.—*Alphitopola maculosa* (magnified).

" Pitchy-brown, pubescent; eyes, labrum, and antennæ brown; palpi pale reddish brown; head and prothorax with five narrow stripes; elytra with rather obscure large tessellated and sometimes nearly confluent white spots; under surface pure white; legs pale brown, with a slight whitish pubescence.　Length, 5 lines."— Pascoe, *loc. cit.*

The small " Longhorn" represented in the figure is noted by Miss Glanville as being " injurious to Orange and Naartje trees in Grahamstown Gardens."

The specimen sent for identification has been kindly compared by Mr. Pascoe with the type of *A. maculosa*, and is regarded by him as a variety of that species, the

ALPHITOPOLA MACULOSA. 33

original description of which is reproduced above. This
specimen differs from the typical *maculosa* in having
the upper side closely covered with a greyish white
tomentum ; the markings on the head, thorax and elytra
are very indistinct and of a dusky-brown colour, and in
places where the tomentum has been removed it is
shining black; the antennæ and legs are red-brown, the
base of the former and the femora are dusky and
densely covered with fine white pubescence. In some
respects it approaches very close to *A. rustica*, Führs.

*Specimens of the above-named beetles in their larval and
chrysalis state, for figuring, and notes of their life-history,
would be very desirable.*

Besides the three foregoing species of "Longhorns,"
Mr. Bairstow observes, "there are numerous other kinds
more or less injurious to timber"; and Miss Glanville
has sent specimens of six other species for determination, but as no special notes accompany them, it would
appear more advisable to defer giving figures and
descriptions of them until some definite information
is obtained concerning their habits and the kind of trees
which they attack. The species sent are as follows:—

FAM. PRIONIDÆ.

ERIODERUS HIRTUS, Fab.

Callidium hirtum, Fab. Ent. Syst. i. 2, p. 324; Oliv.
Ent. iv. 70, p. 5, t. 5, f. 62.
Prionus pallens, Fab. Ent. Syst. Suppl. p. 141.

MACROTOMA DIMIDIATICORNIS, Waterh.

Macrotoma dimidiaticornis, Waterhouse, Ann. Mag. Nat.
Hist. 5, xiv. p. 386.

FAM. LAMIIDÆ.

PHRYNETA SPINATOR, Fab.

Lamia spinator, Fab. Ent. Syst. i. 2, p. 276.

D

Fam. CERAMBYCIDÆ.

Litopus dispar, Thoms.

Litopus dispar, Thomson, Ess. Class. Ceramb. p. 171.

Promeces linearis, Linn.

Leptura linearis, Linn. Syst. Nat. ed. x. p. 399.
Cerambyx fusiformis, DeGeer, Mém. vii. p. 657, t. 49, f. 7.
Saperda longipes, Fab. Syst. Ent. App. p. 824 ; Oliv.
Ent. iv. 70, p. 28, t. 1, f. 8.

Hypocrites mendax, Fåhrs.

Hypocrites mendax, Fåhrs. Ofvers. Kongl. Ak. Forh.,
1872, i. p. 62.

Fam. GALERUCIDÆ.

Iphidea capensis, Baly, n.sp.

Fruit-tree Iphidea.

Specimens of this small Phytophagous beetle have
been examined by Dr. J. S. Baly, and, on its proving to
be a species hitherto undescribed, he has obligingly furnished the technical diagnosis given below* under the
specific name of *capensis.* A more general description
is as follows :—

Of an oblong form, a little widened behind and moderately convex above ; the upper surface and legs of a

* Oblongo-ovata, convexa, flavo-fulva, nitida, pectore abdominisque
nigris, antennis, basi exceptis. tarsisque apice piceis ; thorace lævi ;
elytris tenuiter subcrebre punctatis, margine laterali suturâque anguste
nigris. Long 2 lin.
Hab. South Africa (Grahamstown).
Antennæ more than half the length of the body ; three, four, or five
outer joints nigro-fuscous or black. Thorax smooth, nearly impunctate.
Elytra finely but rather closely punctured. Basal joint of the hinder
tarsi longer than the following three united (J. S. Baly).

pale tawny, or ochreous, yellow, with the eyes, the scutellum, and a very fine marginal line at the suture and sides of the elytra black; the antennæ are pale yellow at the base, and become piceous or black towards the apex ; the tips of the tarsi are also piceous ; on the under side, the head and the sides of the thorax are the same colour as above, the other parts of the body are black. The head is diffusely punctured at the base and has an elevated longitudinal line between the antennæ and a transverse interrupted elevation on the front of the forehead. The thorax is twice as broad at the base as long, a little rounded at the sides and very indistinctly punctured ; in some specimens there is a dark mark on the disk. The scutellum is rounded at the apex and impunctate. The elytra are irregularly and rather closely punctured. The length of the body is 4—5 millm.

Iphidea is closely allied to the genus *Luperus*, of which three species are found rather commonly in England.— O. E. J.

In Miss Glanville's notes this beetle attacks fruit trees (apricot, &c.), swarming over them and devouring leaves and fruit. Observed in Lower Albany, Salem, Orange Grove, and Albany.

For measures of prevention of injury from this insect, details of its life-history are needed ; but (conjecturally) shaking, or sweeping down the beetles when most torpid, and destroying them,—also finding where they hybernate, and clearing these shelters,—would be of use.

Fam. HALTICIDÆ.

DIBOLIA INTERMEDIA, Baly.

Dibolia intermedia, Baly, Trans. Ent. Soc. Lond. 1876, p. 598.

Dark Blue Flea Beetle.

Ovate, very convex above; upper side of a dark and slightly metallic blue; under side black or piceous. The head is very finely and sparingly punctured, with

the front and vertex moderately convex; the antennæ
are nearly half as long as the body, with the first five
or six joints pale fulvous, the other joints are fulvous at
the base and piceous or black at the apex; in some
specimens the three terminal joints are entirely black.
The thorax is more than twice as broad at the base as
long, with the sides rounded and converging from the
base to the apex; the anterior angles are slightly produced, and the surface is distinctly but not very closely
punctured. The scutellum is triangular and smooth.
The elytra are broader than the thorax at the base, and
slightly attenuated towards the apex; they are rather
strongly punctured; some of the punctures are closely
arranged in more or less regular rows on the disk and
sides, but in the interstices and at the apex they are
more remote and confused. The legs are sometimes
entirely black or piceous, but the tibiæ and tarsi are
usually fulvous; the posterior legs have very large
femora, and the tibiæ are channelled above with the
edges of the groove serrate. The length of the body is
2½—3 millm.

The genus *Dibolia* does not occur in Britain; it is
allied to *Psylliodes*, but differs in having eleven-jointed
antennæ, whereas in the latter genus these organs con-
sist of ten joints only. The presence of a bifid spine
at the apex of the posterior tibiæ is the principal
character by which *Dibolia* is distinguished from all the
other genera of *Halticidæ*. In size, colour, and general
aspect this species very much resembles *Psylliodes
chalcomera*, Illig.—O. E. J.

This small "Flea Beetle" has been kindly identified
by Dr. Baly, the well-known authority on this group of
Coleoptera, from specimens sent by Miss Glanville, who
states that it destroys peas and beans at Grahamstown.

Of this and the preceding species (*Iphidea capensis*)
Mr. Bairstow writes that about three years previously
to the date of writing—that is, about 1883—he saw them
in millions right away through British Caffraria, and of

the *Dibolia intermedia* he notes that it used now and then to appear on his apricot trees at Uitenhage.

For reference to remedies found serviceable for this kind of attack, see Index.

ORDER LEPIDOPTERA.

FAM. PAPILIONIDÆ.

PAPILIO DEMOLEUS. (Fig. 17).

Papilio demoleus, Linn. Mus. Lud. Ulr. Reg. p. 214; Cram. Pap. Ex. iii. t. 231, f. A, B; Trimen, Rhopal. Afr. Austr. p. 17, t. 1, f. 1.

FIG. 17.—*Papilio demoleus.*

Common Swallowtail, or Orange Butterfly.

Upper side sooty-black, both the wings, except towards the outer margin, thickly speckled with fine pale yellow scales and with conspicuous pale sulphur-yellow spots and bands. On the front wings there are four or five spots arranged in a semicircle near the middle of the front margin ; beyond these a row of three spots, followed by a smaller elongate spot ; in the middle an irregular transverse band composed of six partially confluent spots, a small one beyond this on the hind margin, a submarginal series of seven round spots, an elongate curved mark near the apex, and eight small spots on the outer margin. The hind wings have a transverse band before the middle in continuation of that on the front wings, a submarginal curved series of seven spots and six smaller ones on the outer margin ; besides these pale sulphur-yellow markings, there is a round eye-like spot composed of fine blue and dull golden scales on the anterior margin, and a similar one, bordered behind by a broad dark red lunular spot, near the anal angle. On the under side both the wings are dark brown, with pale sulphur-yellow markings similar to the upper side, and some additional streaks of the same colour at the base ; on the hind wings there are also eye-like spots similar to those on the upper side, and besides these, there is a sublunular mark of blue and dull golden scales just beyond the middle of the transverse band, and a series of five similar marks before the submarginal row of spots. The under side of the abdomen is ochre-yellow, with four longitudinal black lines. The expanse of the wings is 83—108 millm. (3¼—4¼ in.).— O. E. J.

"*Larva.*—Pale yellowish green, marbled with purple or purplish grey running in irregular sub-transverse markings on the sides. Numerous pale ferruginous, small, ocellate spots sprinkled about purple markings. A broad, longitudinal, white stripe above spiracles. Head and legs pale sandy brown ; as well as two small

pointed tubercles on segment next head, from between
which is protruded, when the animal is irritated, a
crimson, Y-shaped, tentacle-like organ, emitting a very
peculiar pungent odour. Two similar smaller tubercles
on anal segment (but no Y-shaped organ). A very
sluggish larva, and as variable in the distribution of its
colours as the butterfly is constant in its pattern. The
young caterpillar differs strikingly from the full-grown
one, being very dark, without green colouring, and
clothed with short spines. Feeds on *Umbelliferæ*, *Bubon
galbanum*, and *gummiferum*, and in gardens on the fennel.
Also on orange and lemon trees."

Fig. 18.—Larva and pupa of *Papilio demoleus*, L. (after figure given
by Prof. Trimen.)

" *Pupa*.—Dark ash-grey or brownish grey, varied with
darker shades and streaks. Rather elongate ; the bifid
head and thoracic elevation very prominent. Commonly
attached to the older stems of its food-plants, which it
closely resembles in colour."—Trimen, ' Rhopalocera
Africæ Australis,' p. 18.

Of this Mr. Bairstow mentioned :—" This butterfly is
common in gardens nearly all over Eastern Province.
The larva used to swarm in my garden at Uitenhage
(1880-1) on fennel, and the perfect insect was one of the
commonest butterflies. From the conspicuous character
and size of larva it is easily eradicated temporarily by
picking. It prefers fennel to orange."

The following observation was also forwarded from
Mr. de Witt Meulen, of the Winterhoek :—" The larvæ
appear generally at the end of November or beginning
of December, on the leaves of orange trees. The spots
on their green bodies are modified by age. If touched
they emit an odour acrid and very pungent, withdrawing
their feelers at will. They are generally in greater
number on trees the lower branches of which are allowed
to trail on the ground, and if not disturbed may in that
case destroy all the leaves.

" It is advisable to cut all branches of shrubs under
one foot above the ground ; to turn as often as possible
the soil within a circle of one foot from the trunk,
keeping it moist, and to watch for the grubs during the
summer season, inspecting the leaves daily when they
are attacked, and killing the pest before injury is done
to the tree."

FAM. SPHINGIDÆ.

ACHERONTIA ATROPOS, Linn. (Fig. 19.)

Sphinx atropos, Linn. Syst. Nat. (x.) i. p. 490.
A. atropos, Ochs. Schmett. Eur. ii. 231.

**Moth injurious by stealing Honey, caterpillar by
feeding on various kinds of Leafage.**

Whilst these pages were going through press I received
a note from Mr. S. D. Bairstow, of Port Elizabeth,
suggesting that amongst the injurious insects of Cape
Colony it would be well to mention the " Death's Head

Moth," or, as it is sometimes called on this side of the
world, the "Bee Tiger Moth."

The S. African species is the same as that well known
in Britain, and therefore, as the attack was reported (in
this instance) without specimens being sent, I give below
a figure of the British kind, which was drawn for my
'Manual of British Injurious Insects.'

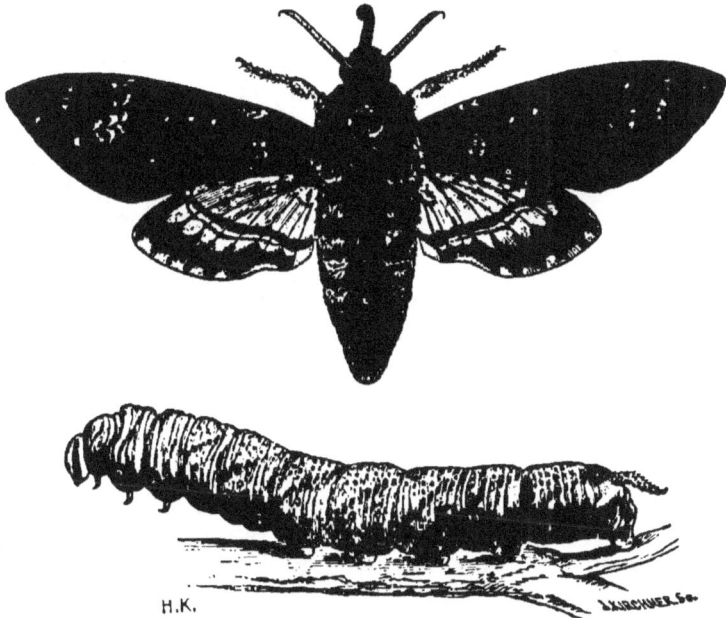

Fig. 19.—*Acherontia atropos.* Death's Head Moth, and caterpillar (less
than natural size, from British specimens).

Mr. Bairstow mentions that in S. Africa (as well as in
other parts of the world) the moth is fond of extracting
the bees' honey from their hives and nests, and he once
found an apparently newly-emerged female clinging with
its fore legs to a honey bees' nest in a bush on the
Zuurberg Pass. He also notes a popular superstition,
amounting to an undoubting belief, that in some way
or other the action of the proboscis has deadly effect.
Various superstitions attach to this moth, partly from

the skull-like marking on its back, partly from the
singular sound or cry which it has the power of giving
forth; and early in the present century, in Campbell's
'Travels in South Africa,' it is stated that the moths
steal honey, . . . "which the Hottentots observing,
in order to monopolise the honey of the wild bees, have
persuaded the colonists that it inflicts a mortal wound."

This beautiful moth is from four to over five inches in
the spread of the wings; the fore wings of a rich brown
varied with yellowish or rusty tints, and with black
towards the base; also with various transverse black
wavy lines, a whitish spot near the centre, and whitish
wavy bars past the middle of the wings, which are likewise sprinkled or irrorated with white. The hinder
wings are of a tawny orange, with two black bands
running parallel to the hinder edge, the widest of these
being nearest the edge of the wing. The head is deep
brown or black, as is also the body between the wings,
which in its velvety down has yellow or pale markings
resembling the shape of a skull. The abdomen is striped
alternately with tawny yellow and black on each segment,
and has a bluish line down the middle.

The caterpillar, which grows to four or five inches in
length, is of various shades of colour, usually reddish at
first, and afterwards yellow or greenish yellow, with
small black warts on the back, and seven stripes placed
slantwise on each side with the upper end pointing
backwards. These are blue, white, and purple in the
centre. The horn at the tail is turned down and
tubercled. The colour of the caterpillar differs with age
and condition, and there is a variety of a mottled brown
colour, which I have once seen, which is very handsome.
Mr. Bairstow mentions of the South African caterpillar
" it is variable, but most commonly brownish." It is also
variable in its food-plants, which include potato
leafage; also they are found in Europe on jasmine,
Datura and *Bignonea catalpa*. Mr. Bairstow mentions
it as being injurious where he has observed it, in
East Province, S. A., to the leafage of vines, or, to use

his own words, it has " a good larval appetite for vine leaves."

In this case there would be little difficulty (conjecturally) in getting rid of it by handpicking, as the great size of the caterpillars causes them to be easily seen, even by faint light at night. In Britain they usually hide by day and come out to feed at night, and when full fed go down under ground to turn to chrysalids, and stirring the surface of the soil deep enough to turn out these chrysalids would be a thorough preventive of recurrence of attack continued from one year to another on vineyards.

No mention is made of means used to stop entrance of the moth into bee-hives, but probably the old-fashioned English method of lessening the size of the entrance just for a time is practised. In any case a lump of clay (or anything not annoying to the tenants), which would make the entrance too small for the enemy to enter, or small enough for the occupiers to defend, would stop thefts.*

FAM. BOMBYCIDÆ,

TRILOCHA FICICOLA (Westw.)   (Fig. 20.)

The specimens figured (p. 44) show the imago, caterpillar, and chrysalis cocoon of a small brownish moth, of which the caterpillars do much damage to the leaves of the fig trees at Port Elizabeth, South Africa. The notes from which the following paper was formed were kindly forwarded to me by Mr. S. D. Bairstow from Port Elizabeth (where the habits of the Fig Moth were

---

* The caterpillars of some other species of the Sphinx moths are injurious to vine leafage in Canada, and, as they may possibly occur in Cape Colony as similarly injurious, it would be well, in case of their occurrence being noticed, to have observations of their habits. These go into chrysalis state respectively underground; in the ground at a moderate depth; amongst rubbish on the ground; in a cell on the surface; or, in one instance, in a light web binding a leaf together; and could be destroyed accordingly.

observed by Mr. Russel Hallack and himself), together
with the specimens from which the figure is taken.   I
should also mention that I am indebted for the specific
name to the excellent authority of Professor Westwood,
who was good enough to examine the specimens which
I submitted to him, and informed me that the species
was "very closely allied to the Eastern *Trilocha varians,*
and may be described under the name of *Trilocha
ficicola.*"

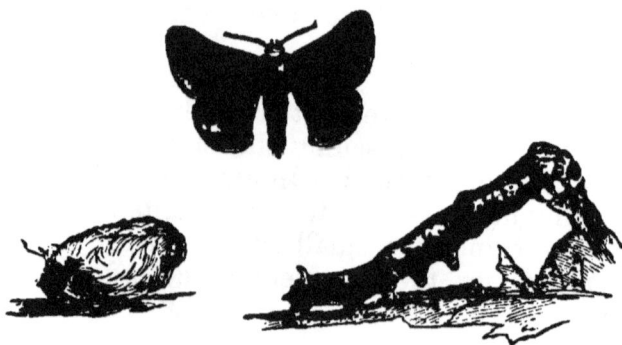

Fɪɢ. 20.—*Trilocha ficicola.*   Fig Moth, caterpillar, and cocoon.*

The caterpillars, which are called hunchbacks, are
distinguished by their pale tawny colour above, and
dark colour below, joining at a line running along the
side.   The dark colour runs up with a point to the
lumps on the back of the caterpillar, and thus adds to
the appearance the grub has (when bent down to feed)
of being humpbacked.   The colours are brightest whilst
the grub is young; when it has got to its full growth of
about an inch and a half long, the dark parts are more
mottled with light, and the light parts with dark marks.
It will also be seen that the grub or caterpillar has a

* The transmitted specimen of imago not preserving the characteristic
markings sufficiently for specified figuring of the fore wings, the reader
is referred, for details of markings and description, to p. 45.

blunt spike pointing upwards above the tail. They do not move about much, but are sluggish and stationary, and when stretched out and merely standing on their sucker feet the colouring and the lumps on the back make them look much like twigs. Besides the harm they do to the leafage, they seem partial to the sprouting buds, and will clear them nearly entirely away, and they seem to prefer destroying the leaves on one tree almost completely before they go on to another that may stand near. In a garden containing about thirty fig-trees seven were found to be attacked, the remainder being free. They feed up quickly, and are very hardy. When full fed the caterpillar spins an oval case (Fig. 20, p. 44) round itself, formed of white silk, which may be found either on the tree or near the roots in the earth. The silk cocoons are of the size of the one figured, and within these the caterpillar throws off its skin and turns to a chrysalis, from which in due time there comes out the little brown and grey Fig Moth.

These moths are about an inch in the spread of the fore wings, which are palish grey, with a broad band of brown along the hinder edge, and a small patch of brown at the end of the wing, and also a brown line on a part of the fore edge, which altogether give a pattern as of a broad, pale grey, forked mark lying on a brown ground towards the front of the wing. The hind wings are chestnut-brown, the down on body chiefly greyish, the eyes pitchy.

The caterpillars watched by Mr. Bairstow in his garden at Port Elizabeth turned to chrysalids from the 26th of June to the 10th of July, and the moths appeared from them after only nine days. There are apparently two broods during the year—they are very prolific.

Prevention and Remedy.

Picking the caterpillars off by hand is considered the best way to get rid of them whilst attack is going on. Very few can be got rid of by trying to shake them from the trees, as the caterpillar is a silk producer, and has great powers of clinging to the leaves, and also of weaving and interweaving silk supports and body bands, but it would be worth trying whether sudden syringing with soft-soap wash would not be of use.

Fowls are said not to help much where they have been tried, for they have been found to nip leaves from the trees, but not to touch the caterpillars, except when they were in motion. They are remarkably free from attacks of parasite insects.

Picking cocoons off the trees, and turning over the soil to throw out such cocoons as are just below the surface or bury others, would lessen the amount of the coming attack; and also, as the moths are noted as being sluggish, it might answer well to shake the trees at whatever time the moths are sleepiest, so that the moths should fall on cloths below, and gather them up and destroy, or trample them on the ground as they fall.—E. A. O.

FAM. TINEIDÆ.

PLUTELLA CRUCIFERARUM, Zell. (Fig. 21.)

Plutella cruciferarum, Zeller, Stett. Ent. Zeit. 1843, p. 281.*

Diamond-back Moth.

The front wings are long and narrow, greyish brown, darker towards the centre, but paler and marked with some small brown spots in front; a rather broad whitish or ochreous grey band along the hinder margin, with three rounded projections on its front edge: this band is usually spotted with very small dark points, and in some specimens it is considerably obscured by the ground colour on the hinder margin, leaving the three projecting parts alone conspicuous. The hind wings are narrow and pointed at the apex, have a long fringe,

---

* For the identification of this small moth (rather a difficult matter, from the injured state in which the specimens were sent) I am indebted to the kindness of Lord Walsingham.—E. A. O.

and are of a pale ashy grey colour. The body and legs are brownish grey; the head and thorax grey or ochreous grey; the antennæ are brown, finely spotted with white. The expanse of the wings is 14—16 millm.

When this moth is at rest the front wings meet along the back, and the projecting parts of the pale bands form diamond-shaped marks, whence the English name of " Diamond-back Moth."

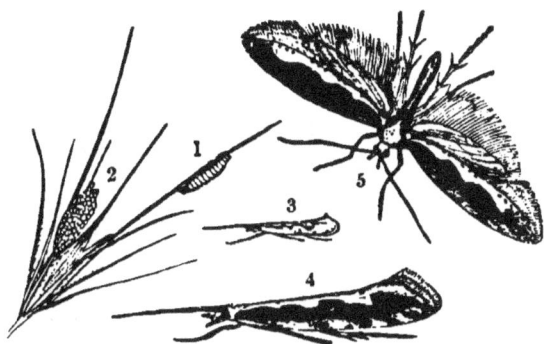

Fig. 21.—*Plutella cruciferarum.* Moth (natural size and magnified), caterpillar, and cocoon.

A piece of cabbage-leaf, much injured by the workings of the caterpillars, was sent over by Mr. Bairstow as a sample of the damage caused by them : specimens of the moths and caterpillars were also sent, together with the following note by Mr. J. de Witt Meulen, of the Winterhoek :—

" Larvæ very numerous on young cabbage-plants in June and July. Those placed in breeding-boxes covered themselves, within three days, with a thin translucent web, and remained about thirty days in the chrysalis state. . . . Heavy rains or frequent watering of the leaves destroys many grubs. If planted in rows, cabbages are protected on each side by a line covered with glue or molasses ; many moths are prevented thereby depositing their eggs on the plants."

Mr. de Witt Meulen also mentioned that the larvæ collected by him in the beginning of August,—that is in the S. African winter (corresponding in time of year with the height of summer here),—did not develop into moths, but "gnats" only (Ichneumon flies, from which it would appear that this attack must be much kept down by parasites, S. D. B.) appeared instead. The June and August presence of caterpillars would correspond with that of the first and second brood in Germany, which are thus described by Dr. E. L. Taschenberg :—

"The sixteen-footed caterpillars are attenuated at each end, of a bright green, and sprinkled with small bristles, but of which the wart-like bases can only be seen when much magnified. The head is black. Length, 7 mm. At the beginning of June ; for the second time in August and September, under a thin web at the back of the leaves of many different kinds of plants of the cabbage tribe, both wild and cultivated."*

Specimens of cocoons containing the chrysalids were needed to complete the S. African set ; but from the identity of the species and similarity of its habits, in all that was reported, with those of the Diamond-back Moth of Europe (Fig. 21, p. 47), it may be presumed also that the caterpillar goes into chrysalis, as in Europe, in a cocoon spun on the food-plant or on the ground.

For prevention of attack, if it is practicable—as mentioned by Mr. de Witt Meulen— to place sticky material so as to trap the moths, this would of course be desirable ; also where a crop has been destroyed, or weeds near a crop are much infested, it would be well to collect the injured remains before the moths came out of the chrysalids and destroy them. Burning of course would be the surest way, but, as it is the nature of the chrysalis to go through its changes in a more or less open web exposed to air and changes of weather, probably ploughing in of the infested remains would be sufficient treatment, *if done before the moths developed.*

* See 'Praktische Insekten Kunde,' by Dr. E. L. Taschenberg, pt. III. p. 273.

For this purpose observation is needed of how long the chrysalis state lasts. Mr. de Witt Meulen mentions it as lasting thirty days with the August specimens. In Europe it is noted as about eighteen days with the first brood, and that the second hybernates.

For remedy, the only applications which appear to answer are nitrate of soda or such dressings or treatment as may push on growth, or mechanical means, which sometimes answer. Sweeping the infested plants with light boughs fixed to a scuffler, or sending a man through the crop to shake the caterpillars off with a bough, whilst a boy accompanying throws any mixture of caustic lime or soot on them, has been found to answer; or sending sheep through the field is of use, by fairly knocking or pushing the caterpillars off, or causing them to throw themselves down, when many are trodden to death by the animals.

This attack is one which from time to time attracts attention in Britain as very injurious.

ORDER DIPTERA.

FAM. MUSCIDÆ.

SUB-FAM. TRYPETINÆ.

CERATITIS CITRIPERDA, Macl. (Fig. 22.)

Ceratitis citriperda, MacLeay, Zool. Journ. iv. p. 475, t. 15, fig.
Tephritis capitata, Wied. Analect. Entom. p. 55.
Trypeta capitata, Wied. Aussereur. Zweifl. Ins. ii. p. 496.
Petalophora capitata, Macq. Dipt. ii. p. 454.
? Ceratitis hispanica, Brême, Ann. Soc. Ent. Fr. 1842, p. 183, t. 7, f. 1—5.

E

Orange Fly ("Trypeta" Fly, S. A.).

The "Orange Fly" has long been well known as causing great amount of damage to oranges, and likewise as attacking some other kinds of fruit, including peaches.

The insect appears to be very widely distributed, as it is stated by various observers and writers, from the time of Latreille and MacLeay onwards, to be found in the Azores, the Cape de Verd Islands, Madeira, Mauritius, and countries on the Indian Ocean, and if, as considered by Dr. Schiner,* the only European kind (the *Ceratitis Hispanica*, Brême), brought from Andalusia by M. Rambur and described by the Marquis de Brême in the Annals of the French Entomological Society) is identical with the *C. citriperda* of MacLeay, this adds the South of Europe to its geographical range.

Fig. 22.—*Ceratitis citriperda*, Fly, magnified, showing the form of the head filaments. Outline, natural size.

On the 5th of July, 1888, Mr. J. B. Hellier wrote to me from Grahamstown, S. Africa, regarding the attacks of this very destructive fruit fly as follows :—

* " Die einige europaische Art, *Ceratitis hispanica*, Brême ('Ann. de la Soc. Entom. de France,' I. ii. 183, Tfl. 7, I. 1—5) durfte mit *Trypeta capitata*, Wiedem., oder *Ceratitis citriperda*, MacLeay, identisch sein, obwohl die *Wiedemann*'sche Art aus Isle de France, und den Azoren stammt."—' Fauna Austriaca, Die Fliegen,' von J. Rudolph Schiner, Pt. II., p. 174.

"Enclosed please find a specimen of a fly, which has become a most serious pest to our fruit-growers and most objectionable to our fruit-eaters.

"In some districts last year, Albany amongst the rest, four-fifths of our peaches, apricots, figs, and plums were uneatable.

"The perfect insect may be seen flying about very swiftly, and depositing some half-dozen eggs in a fruit.

"They do not deposit their eggs till the fruit is turning ripe—that is, getting sweet. The maggots are never found in green apricots used for making pies, neither are they found in sour apples.

"The season 1886-87 was remarkable for the freedom of the fruit from maggots. The oranges at Uitenhage in October and November, 1886, were infested and maggotty, but the apricots and peaches which came ripe in December and January were comparatively free. My idea was that the mild weather with spring rain brought out the flies, but, there being no other ripe fruit than oranges, the maggots did not come to flies in the usual way. Oranges in our early spring time are at the best, being then thoroughly ripe and lusciously sweet.

"The fly and three cocoons sent were obtained from an infested peach; there were six maggots; two flies came out of the cocoons—one escaped, and one of the larvæ did not become a pupa. The other three cocoons are enclosed." . . . . "It is more injurious than the Codlin Moth, or in fact any other fruit destroyer."

"I have not been able to make out to my satisfaction the way in which the flies are perpetuated from year to year,—whether they hybernate like house-flies, or whether they lie dormant in the cocoons."—J. B. H.

I had the advantage of being able to show Mr. Hellier's specimens to Prof. J. O. Westwood, Life President of our Royal Entomological Society, who has himself personally studied the habits of this fly as far as can be done from imported specimens. He identified the imago as without doubt a male specimen of the *Ceratitis citriperda*, and drew my attention to the presence of the peculiar slender

filaments, knobbed or dilated at the extremity, which are
placed on the head between the eyes, and which are a
characteristic of the male of this fly.

Prof. Westwood, in his paper on this "Orange Fly,"
in the No. of the 'Gardener's Chronicle' for Sept. 9,
1848, thus describes the fly :—

"The perfect insect is one of the most beautiful of the
order to which it belongs, its general colour being fulvous
buff, with the thorax grey spotted with black ; the scutellum black, with an undulated white line at the base,
and two pale grey bars across the abdomen ; the basal
half of the wing is much variegated with minute black
dots and streaks, with a buff and ashy cloud near the
base, another across the middle, another along the
extremity of the fore margin dotted with black, and an
ashy bar on the inner margin. The male is singularly
distinguished by having two slender filaments arising
between the eyes, knobbed at the tips (as represented in
the figure), a peculiarity which we believe is possessed
by no other dipterous insect, and which is wanting in
the female."

In the specimen sent me this peculiar growth might
be exactly described, in the words of Macquart, as a,
filament terminated by a rhomboidal plate.*

With regard to the maggot of this fly Prof. Westwood
writes, in the paper quoted above :—

"The larva is a white fleshy grub, destitute of legs,
very similar to that of the celery-stem fly, and, like it,
it possesses two small black contiguous hooks at the
front of the body, which it alternately protrudes and
retracts, thereby tearing the delicate membrane in which
the drops of juice are contained. The body is gradually
attenuated in front, very indistinctly articulated ; the
anterior segments, including the head, are retractile.
There are generally several of these larvæ in each
orange, and when removed and placed upon a flat surface

* *Petalophora capitata. Trypeta capitata,* 'Wied. Auss. Zweif.' No. 3.
' Histoire Naturelle des Diptères,' par M. Macquart, vol. ii. p. 454.

they have the power of springing to a considerable distance, in the same manner as the well-known Cheese Maggot. When full grown they eat their way out of the orange, and undergo the change to the pupa state on the outside.

"The pupa is a small, hard, brown, oval body, the outer surface scarcely indicating any traces of articulation, being the dried skin of the larva, within which the real pupa is enclosed."—J. O. W.

No larvæ (or maggots) were forwarded, but the pupa or chrysalis case, of which several were sent, corresponded with the above description.

In regard to method of attack and various points of life history it was considered by Prof. Westwood, from examination of imported oranges, that the presence of infestation might be inferred sometimes by a puncture not larger than that made by a pin, "but generally surrounded by a withered and discoloured spot varying in size from that of a sixpence to a half-crown." "On opening the orange the interior beneath the discoloured space is found to be decayed, and in the middle of this decaying mass the maggot is to be found."

From notes placed in my hands by Mr. Hellier regarding this fly (now generally known as the Trypeta Fly in the infested district) it appears that, some seven or eight years ago, the mischief attracted the attention of the Albany Natural History Society (when he gave the result of his investigations), and later on (in 1874) he again reported on the subject. In order to be sure of the species of insect giving rise to the mischief, "a collection was made of the various kinds of fruit chiefly infested, consisting of apricots, peaches, pears, apples, and figs. The fruits containing the maggots were placed under glass shades. In the course of three or four days, or a week, according to their age, they changed into the chrysalis or pupa state. In ten days from the time they assumed the pupa state the perfect insect appeared. The fly was exactly the same in whatever fruit the insect was bred."

It is further mentioned that the pest is a "day-light" fly, which is a serviceable matter to know relatively to preventive measures.

The only known method of preserving fruit from this attack appears to be protecting it by tying it up in calico or muslin bags : thus the fruit has been found to escape attack and be free from maggots; but the plan is not practicable on the scale of orchard growing, and, in regard to its habits on the bushes, Prof. Westwood, in the paper above mentioned (quoting from various observers specified), mentions that in the Island of Mauritius it was found generally by M. Desjardins on the leaves of the orange. Also that Dr. Heineker, who found the insect in Madeira, "observed it at rest as though basking, and with the wings expanded on the leaves of some thick shrubs." "It had the manners and appearance of an insect of very confined locomotive power and activity," and he seldom saw it upon the wing farther than passing from shrub to shrub.

One main point of information that is wanted to check attack is—Where does the maggot in *natural circumstances undergo its changes to the chrysalis state?*

In various observations, taken from gathered or imported fruit, the change has taken place inside or upon the fruit; but in the case of the "Apple Maggot" of America,—the *Trypeta pomonella*, Walsh,—which, as a fruit-feeder and one of the *Trypetidæ*, may be conjectured to be very similar to the S. African fly in its habits, the change is recorded by Matthew Cooke and Prof. Saunders, and also by Prof. Lintner, as taking place in the earth. It is stated by Prof. Saunders that—"When about to change the maggot leaves the apple, and, falling to the ground, burrows under the surface and there enters the chrysalis state, in which condition it remains until the middle of the following summer, when the perfect insect escapes in the form of a four-winged fly."*

* 'Insects Injurious to Fruit,' by Prof. Saunders, p. 135. Philadelphia, 1883.

Having been specially requested to offer some suggestions as to means of lessening this attack I endeavour
to do so, but at the same time must beg my readers to
bear in mind that, as I have not technical knowledge of
the S. African methods of fruit growing, I am only able
to suggest on the general principles of prevention which
are applicable everywhere.

It is plain that a large proportion of the maggots
causing the attack come to maturity very rapidly in the
ripe fruit. If this infested fruit can be distinguished
from the sound, might not some proportion of it be
hand-picked, and thus much future infestation be got
rid of ? Fruit need not be dead ripe for many household
purposes, and with a little management much of the
infested fruit might be utilized. No information is given
as to whether the infested fruit matures sooner and falls
more easily than the sound : if it did so, gentle shaking
of the trees, and turning sheep or pigs on in case of
orchard infestation, would clear off the fruit and all the
contained pests immediately. But investigation appears
to be needed as to whether this " Orange " or so-called
" *Trypeta* " Fly is double-brooded. Mention is made
that the flies hybernate in small numbers. Is it not
possible, as with very many other insect attacks, that
the second brood may differ in habits, and that the
maggots of this may hybernate in maggot or chrysalis
state just below the surface of the earth, and come out
in fly condition in what is the following spring of the
S. African season ?

It might be found out very easily whether the maggots
drop to the ground, by laying cloths smeared with any
sticky material which would prevent them straying away
beneath a few of the infested trees,—and this I think
would be particularly desirable with regard to apple
Trypeta attack. It might *possibly* prove on investigation
that some at least of this was originated by importation
of the American *Trypeta pomonella*, which, though of a
different genus, is of the same family, and certainly
similar in some of its habits.

. If the flies are sluggish and inactive, when basking on the leaves, their numbers might be reduced by shaking them down on sticky cloths, or by syringings with good soft soap or whale oil soap washes, which is an American remedy.

Any fruit that is infested should not be allowed to remain on the ground to continue attack, and if on investigation it should prove that the later maggots go into chrysalis state in the ground, or even that a large proportion of them do so,—or if it could be found where the flies usually hibernate,—these points would help greatly in lessening amount of attack.

FAM. HIPPOBOSCIDÆ (EPROBOSCIDEA).

HIPPOBOSCA STRUTHIONIS, n. sp.* (Fig. 23.)

FIG. 23.—*Hippobosca struthionis*, and egg-like pupa-case, nat. size and magnified ; foot and claw magnified.

Ostrich Fly.

The head is impressed and dull black in the middle, the sides next the eyes shining yellow; the vertex is

* *Hippobosca struthionis*, n. sp.—Nigra, nitida; capite medio opaco, lateribus flavo-marginatis, clypeo flavo, postice rotundato, integro; thorace obsolete strigoso, maculis quatuordecim flavis, postice transversim impresso, strigoso ; scutello macula media flava ; abdomine opaco griseo-hirsuto; pedibus nigro-piceis, griseo-hirsutis, tibiarum medio flavo-notato, tarsis rufo-piceis, femoribus anticis subtus ad basin rufoflavis. Exp. alar. 16—18 mm. (O. E: Janson).
HAB. Mount Stewart, S. Africa.

very smooth, shining black, and narrowly bordered with yellow behind; the clypeus is pale yellow, with the centre and margins brownish; it is deeply notched in front, broadly rounded behind, and has a deep central impression near the base; the antennæ are black, with brown setæ; the proboscis black, with long grey setæ; eyes pale brown. The thorax is deep shining black, with fourteen small yellow spots; it is very feebly and irregularly striated on the disk, but more distinctly so at the sides; there are two slight impressions in front, and a deep, transversely striated, depression behind. The scutellum is shining black, with a triangular pale yellow spot in the centre; there are some long grey setæ on the hind margin, and in some specimens there is an additional small yellow spot on each side. The abdomen is finely granulate, dull black, with long grey hairs. The underside and legs are black or pitchy-black, with long grey hairs; the knees and tarsi are pitchy-red; the underside of the anterior femora are yellow at the base, and there is a yellow or reddish yellow spot in the middle of all the tibiæ. The wings are pale brownish hyaline, with the veins pitchy-red or nearly black. The expanse of the wings is 16—18 millm.

As this species was found to differ from all others existing in accessible collections, and not to agree with any published description, specimens were submitted to Mons. Bigot, of Paris, an eminent authority on the Diptera, and he, after a careful examination, pronounces it to be a species hitherto undescribed.

It is somewhat remarkable that this fly should have escaped observation until quite recently, and prove to be a species apparently unknown to naturalists, as it is said to have been found in great abundance in the district in which it occurs.

Another species of these flies (*Hippobosca rufipes*, Wied.*) has been recorded as occurring on the wild ostrich many years since, but, according to the observations of Lichtenstein during his travels in South Africa,

* 'Aussereurop. Zweiflügl. Insecten,' vol. ii. p. 604 (1830).

this species infests the quagga, and is introduced on to the ostrich by the frequent intermingling of the herds of these birds and animals.—O. E. J.

With regard to what may be appropriately called the "Ostrich Flies," Mr. Bairstow wrote me, on the 20th of May, 1886, as follows :—" . . . I send herewith three or four flies from the pigeon " [figured and described in following paper—E. A. O.], " and a lot of larger ones with " (what were considered to be) " eggs of the insect. They were sent me through an up-country correspondent, Mr. J. H. Cawood, of Mount Stewart," who further reported that there were thousands on the (ostriches), and that they irritated the birds so that half of their time was taken up in pecking at the flies, and that, judging from the increase in the last two years, if something was not done to destroy them, the feathers would not be worth sending to market, and the writer believed that in time they would destroy the birds.

With this communication specimens of the flies from the ostriches were forwarded, together with several of the so-called eggs,—really pupa-cases which were laid by the flies after they had been placed in the bottle in which they were sent. None of these egg-like pupæ were found on the birds.

Mr. Bairstow remarked that this appeared to be a terrible pest, and well worth investigating, and later on forwarded me more specimens, with the mention that they were a very serious trouble,—appearing (as he correctly describes the habits of this kind of fly) " to use both suckers and claws to irritate the bird, causing it to peck and injure the feathers, especially those of the wing, which are the most valuable."

These observations are of especial interest, as, with the exception of the flies recorded (as mentioned previously) on some wild ostriches, it had been considered that the *Hippobosca* only attacked quadrupeds. The very peculiar life-history of these flies—that is, of the *Hippoboscidæ*—may perhaps throw some light on the means of checking their increase. They do *not* lay eggs; neither, as is the case with some flies, produce living maggots, but the maggot lives and feeds inside the abdomen of the female fly until it is full grown; then it forms a kind of roundish, white or yellowish, case, which is deposited by the fly, and in this case the maggot changes to the pupa or chrysalis state, from which the fly presently comes out. How soon this happens would be useful to know, and might easily be found out by putting some of the cases in a box in tolerably natural temperature and watching for appearance.

The cases sent me were much like little roundish white balls, with a brown spot on one side: it is very likely that they would be found shortly to turn, like those of the European *Hippobosca* examined, found on horses and cattle, to a black colour.

As Mr. Cawood mentions that he did not find any of these cases on the infested ostriches,—and it is quite plain that it was laying time with the flies, for I saw cases they had laid, with them in the bottle,—it may fairly be presumed that a large proportion of them fall to the ground; and here we get to what might be a measure of prevention.

If the ostriches remain on the ground where the fly-cases have fallen, it is almost certain when the flies come out of the cases that they will start a new attack; but if ground could be changed so that a dressing of quick-lime, or anything that would kill the contents of the cases, could be run over the ground, and the birds individually dressed so as to remove at least a good proportion of the flies, so that they should not infest the new ground, this would appear likely to lessen the amount of attack greatly.

If any poultry can safely be allowed to run on ostrich fields or folds, these might probably be turned to good account in picking up the egg-like fly-cases which drop from amongst the ostrich feathers, especially when the cases are still white.

The European kind of fly (*Hippobosca equina*) usually

collects on special parts of the infested animal; and like the Ostrich Fly causes irritation both by blood-sucking and creeping, which it can do in any direction, sideways or backwards, with great nimbleness, as well as forwards, and the remedies used are local applications or dressings. These are of any kind that will make the part obnoxious to the fly,—tobacco decoctions, soapsuds, and various other things are found to succeed ; but of course there is not the difficulty in the case of stock that there is with the ostriches as to spoiling beauty of feathers. I know McDougall's dip has been used for Ostrich Fly, but have not yet had report of result. The remedy applied by Mr. Cawood, of sulphuring the infested birds, would, on general principle of treatment of insect attack to fowls, appear likely to be useful,

In treatment for " Forest Fly," the European kind before referred to, it has been found that the great point to check increase is the most careful attention to *cleanliness :* the flies increase most rapidly on animals that have been neglected, or in which state of health, condition, or other circumstances of welfare or surroundings, disposes them to *attract* the flies, and to suffer specially when they come.

No details are given of whether the attack lasts all the year, or begins from flies which have spent the winter in shelters, or have come out of the chrysalis in the spring ; but if this latter is what happens, it could not fail to be of service to use all measures available, such as whitewashing or cleaning out what might be exceedingly likely to shelter, in any sheds or houses, or places used for collecting or sheltering, or artificial hatching of the ostriches, the chrysalids or the flies which presently would start new attack on the birds.

OLFERSIA SPINIFERA, Leech. (Fig. 24.)

Feronia spinifera, Leech, Mem. Wern. Nat. Hist. Soc. ii.
   p. 557, t. 26, f. 1—3.
Olfersia spinifera, Wied. Aussereur. Zweifl. Ins. ii. p. 607 ;
   Wulp, Tidj. v. Ent. xxiii. p. 193.

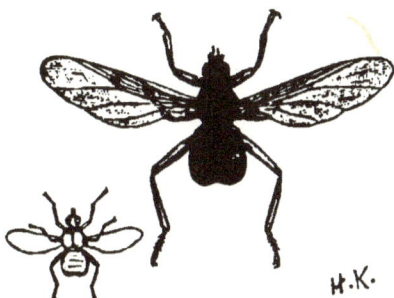

FIG. 24.—*Olfersia spinifera*, nat. size and magnified.*

Pigeon Fly.

In structure and general form this species is very
similar to the Ostrich Fly (*H. struthionis*), but it is a
rather smaller and an altogether more slender insect.
The head is narrower, and more closely attached to the
thorax, dull brown or piceous in the middle, the base and
sides next the eyes shining ; the clypeus is brownish
yellow, shining, and has a large central notch in front.
The thorax is much narrower than in *H. struthionis*,
piceous or black, and without spots ; the anterior angles
are furnished with a large pointed tubercle, which
projects in front outside the back part of the eyes ; these
tubercles and the sides of the thorax are usually paler
than the other parts, and in some specimens are of a
very pale greenish, or yellowish, brown. The scutellum
is very short, transverse, and smooth ; it varies in colour

---

* In the magnified figure the middle pair of legs are partially hidden
by the wings.—E. A. O.

from yellowish brown to pitchy-black. The abdomen is dull black or piceous, with short grey hairs; the sides and base are usually paler, and sometimes yellowish brown. The wings are narrower and more pointed at the apex than in *H. struthionis*, with the nervures finer, and there are three distinct nervures crossing the wing obliquely to the hind margin. The legs vary in colour from piceous-brown to pale brownish yellow; the claws are black, and differ from those of *Hippobosca* in being acutely bidentate from the base; the inner tooth is as fine and nearly as long as the outer one; the feet thus appear to have four ungues, or claws, on each. The head, thorax, apex of the abdomen and the femora have, besides the pubescence, some long brown bristles or setæ. The expanse of the wings is 13—15 millm.— O. E. J.

The specimens sent over of the fly described and figured above were taken from tame pigeons by Mr. J. Crawford, of Port Elizabeth, and similar flies are said to be found on wild birds. These being (like the Ostrich Flies mentioned previously) of the family of the *Hippoboscidæ,* they have the same method of increase, and similar principles of treatment would be applicable to keeping down great amount of infestation.—E. A. O.

Order ORTHOPTERA.

Fam. ACRIDIIDÆ.

Phymateus morbillosus (Linn.) (Fig. 25.)

Gryllus morbillosus, Linn. Syst. Nat. ii. p. 700 ; Roesel. Ins. ii. t. 18, f. 6.

Locust.

The head and thorax are either entirely bright vermilion-red or pale yellow or greenish, with the raised lines and

FIG. 25.—*Phymateus morbillosus.*

tubercles red. The head is sparsely punctured, and has four raised longitudinal lines in front; the two central lines are close together and very prominent between the antennæ, but diverge and curve outwardly towards the eyes on the front of the forehead; the vertex is convex, and has a slight raised longitudinal line in the centre; the antennæ are composed of about twenty joints and taper slightly towards the apex, the basal joint is thick and pale yellow, the second is very short and reddish yellow or pitchy, the other joints are deep black and finely punctured. The thorax has large tubercles on the upper part in front, and some smaller ones behind and at the sides; there is a raised longitudinal line in the centre, interrupted by four transverse impressed lines; the basal part is punctured or rugose, and is considerably raised and produced behind. The base of the wings and the intervening part of the body is dark brown or black. The abdomen is yellow, with the base of each segment broadly margined with black at the sides and above. The fore wings vary in different individuals from indigo-blue or purple to pale greenish yellow; the short transverse nervules are spotted with yellow. The hind wings are of a similar colour to the fore wings in front, and have numerous small dark purple or blackish spots; the hinder part varies in different individuals from pale pinkish yellow to bright vermilion, and the spots are smaller and less numerous than in front. The legs vary from yellow to vermilion, with the knees, the tips of the spines on the tibiæ, and the tarsi, more or less purple or pitchy black. The underside of the body is yellow. The expanse of the wings varies from 90 to 140 millim. ($3\frac{1}{2}$—$5\frac{1}{2}$ in.).

This fine locust is very variable both as regards colour and size; the highly coloured individuals in which the vermilion predominates are exceedingly gorgeous insects. It occurs as far as the River Congo in West Africa, and is said to be also found in Madagascar.—O. E. J.

Unfortunately the few lines of observation sent from

S. Africa regarding the above species, and likewise regarding the *C. ruficornis* noted below, were too general to be of any definite service as to their habits or measures of prevention. I am only able, therefore, at present to add a figure of the very beautiful specimen of the *P. morbillosus* which was sent me, and to suggest that notes of the life-history of both species would be of much interest.—E. A. O.

Another species of Locust received from S. Africa is *Cyrtacanthacris ruficornis*, Fab.: this, in general appearance, resembles the common Egyptian Locust (*Acridium peregrinum*, Oliv.), which likewise occurs in S. Africa.—O. E. J.

ORDER RHYNCHOTA.

DIVISION HOMOPTERA.

FAM. CERCOPIDÆ.

PTYELUS GROSSUS, Fab. (Fig. 26).

Cercopis grossa, Fab. Ent. Syst. iv. p. 47.
Plinthacrus maculicollis, Spin. Gen. d'Ins. Art. p. 154.
P. 4-maculatus, Spin. l. c., p. 155.
Ptyelus eburncus, Walk. List Homopt. iii. p. 704.
P. fabricii, Stål, Ofvers. Vet. Ak. Forhl. 1855, p. 96.
P. hottentottus, Stål l. c., p. 96.

FIG. 26.—*Ptyelus grossus* natural size, and hind leg magnified.

F

Tree Froghopper.

The head is short, broad, prominent, and obtuse in front; the eyes are narrow and oblique on the upper side. The thorax is of a transverse triangular form, with the apex rounded and broadly notched in front of the scutellum; the front margin is a little rounded, and the lateral angles are very acute; the entire surface is very closely and finely punctured, and has sparse short pale pubescence. The scutellum is triangular, with the apex produced and very acute; the punctuation and pubescence are similar to that on the thorax, and there is a large depression in the middle. The tegmina* are broadest about one-third from the base; the costal margin is strongly arched, and the apex is rounded. The legs are rather slender; the hinder tibiæ have two sharp spines on the outer side, and a row of spines on the under side at the apex; there is also a similar row of smaller spines on the first and second joints of the hinder tarsi.

The colour and markings are subject to considerable variation, and several forms, which had been described as distinct species, have since been united by Stål† as simple colour-varieties of *grossus*. In the variety figured the body is of a pale yellow or somewhat ivory colour, with the disk of the thorax and the apex of the abdomen beneath reddish; there are some small black spots at the base of the head and on the front of the thorax, and some larger confluent spots on the hinder part of the thorax and sides of the scutellum; the eyes are dusky brown; the abdomen blackish brown above, with the margins of the segments and some very small spots pale yellow; the tegmina are dusky brown, with two large spots in front, and some very small ones—chiefly towards the base and hind margin—pale yellow; the wings are clear hyaline in front and at the abdominal margin, the middle and outer parts are smoky brown,

---

* Hemelytra, or front wings.
† 'Hemiptera Africana,' iv. p. 71 (1866).

the nervures dark brown; the apex of the rostrum, a broad ring on the anterior tibiæ, the four anterior tarsi, and the spines and claws of the hinder legs, are blackish brown. In other varieties the tegmina are more extensively marked with yellow, or the ground colour is pale yellow, with confluent, undulating, dusky brown markings; the dark spots on the head and thorax vary in size and form, and are sometimes altogether absent; in some specimens the dark ring on the anterior tibiæ is wanting, and the yellow markings on the upper side of the abdomen are often more extensive than in the variety figured.

The length of the body is 12—15 millm., the expanse of the tegmina 30—40 millm.—O. E. J.

Of this handsome insect Miss Glanville, after mentioning that she is doubtful whether this Froghopper may rank among the pests, remarks, " It has been sent from Lower Albany on the plea that it destroys fruit trees. In its larval state it is always enclosed in froth: the trees affected by it are called ' weeping trees,' for clear drops of water are continually distilling from the patches of froth. It is said that a tree attacked dies in a year or two, because the sap is abstracted; but the evidence is by no means conclusive."—M. G.

The habit of the *Cercopidæ*, the family to which this large Froghopper belongs, is to live in all stages by drawing the sap from their food-plants by means of their rostrum or beak. The insects are much the same in shape throughout their lives, but at first (that is, in the larval stage) have no wings; as pupæ the wings are only partly formed. In these stages some kinds live in a mass of froth; and it is noted of one species, *Aphrophora Goudotii*, Bennett, found on trees in Madagascar, that the larva " has the power of emitting a considerable quantity of clear water, especially in the middle of the day, when the heat is greatest." *

* 'Introd. to Classification of Insects,' by Prof. J. O. Westwood, vol. ii., p. 433.

Where " Froghoppers " are numerous they are likely to cause much mischief to the shoots which they frequent, by drawing away sap, and they also do harm by means of the many small punctures caused by inserting their suckers in the tender tissues.

Sometimes they occur on grass (as in the case of the *Ptyelus lineatus,* Linn., which was reported as being very prevalent, in June of last year, on grass in meadows and pastures, at a locality in New York State, U. S. A.*).

The best method of prevention would be to find where the eggs are laid, and destroy them. By keeping close watch on trees usually infested, it would be found whether the young Hoppers (wingless and very minute) were first seen on the branches and shoots, or were found at the lowest part of the trunk, as if crawling up from below. This would probably be a guide as to the class of preventive measures needed—whether stirring the soil, sticky-banding the lower part of the trees, or cleaning the rough bark and dressing it so as to kill vermin in crannies.

In England it has been found a good way of getting rid of the Hop Froghopper, the *Euacanthus interruptus* (which is also one of the *Cercopidæ*, and sometimes very mischievous on hops), to place a light metal tray or piece of iron with a rim three inches high, well smeared with wet tar close to the infested bines, one on each side ; and on the bines being shaken, the Hoppers, taking their great jumps in all directions, simply fell into the tar, and thus a deal both of present and future mischief was got rid of. Where infested fruit trees are not of any great size, the plan of shaking or jarring, so as to make the Hoppers leap on to cloths, or anything below, smeared with wet tar, or with soft soap and paraffin, or with anything that would poison or catch the insects, would be likely to act well.—E. A. O.

---

* 'Fourth Report on Injurious Insects of the State of New York,' by Dr. J. A. Lintner, State Entomologist. Albany, 1888.

FAM. COCCIDÆ.

ICERYA PURCHASI, Mask. (Fig. 27.)

Icerya purchasi, Maskell, Trans. Proc. N. Zealand Inst.
xi. p. 221, t. 8, f. 20, 21.

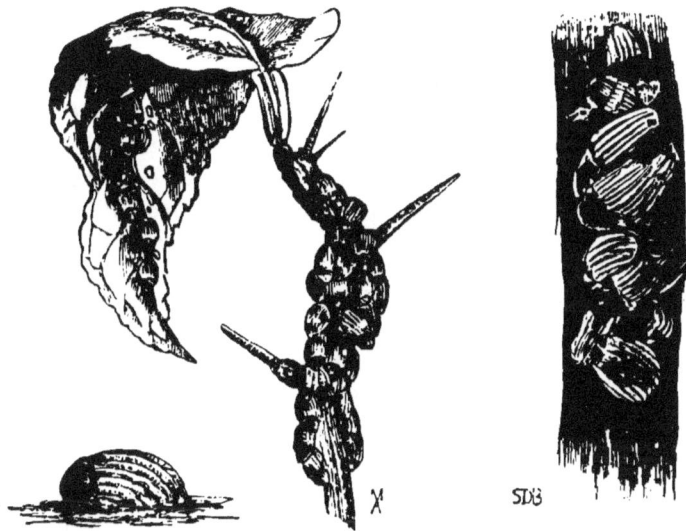

FIG. 27.—*Icerya Purchasi* (female), much magnified; group, magnified
S. African; group on twig and leaf, rather less than life-size
N. American (after fig. by Mrs. Comstock).

*The first edition of this paper was published in 1887,
as a separate pamphlet, under the title of the* 'Australian
Bug of South Africa,' *but this has now been entirely
issued, save one or two copies in the hands of the writer.
Therefore I reprint it now in somewhat abridged form,
excepting with regard to the applications which have been
found of use in destroying the pest. These are repeated,
as the serviceableness of soft soap application, as one of the
best insecticides in this case, has since been confirmed, both
in S. Africa and—by a vast series of experiments—in the
United States of America.*

For practical work (for which this notice is intended) it is hoped that the many figures, and the general description of the female from the S. African specimens which were kindly identified for me as of the Icerya purchasi (Mask.), by M. Signoret, Paris, will be sufficient : those who desire full description will find it in the works referred to below.*

"Australian Bug." Cottony Cushion Scale.

The soft, cushiony, white-ribbed Scale insects, commonly known as the Australian Bug (the Cottony Cushion Scale of North America), rank amongst the most destructive of the insect pests hurtful to trees and shrubs in S. Africa, although little more than fifteen years have elapsed since this pest was first observed in the Colony.

Prof. Roland Trimen, F.R.S., Curator of the South African Museum, mentions, in his Report of 1877, that he first saw the Australian Bug in the Botanic Garden at Cape Town in the latter half of 1873, and "the insect gradually extended its range into all the suburbs of the town."

In 1877 the "Bug" had spread to such an extent, in all parts of the Eastern Province of Cape Colony, as to give rise to an application, from horticulturists and others, to Prof. Trimen for information as to the nature and habits of the new pest, in reply to which request the Report above referred to was prepared.† Local laws and regulations were drawn up with a view to stopping the onward spread of this destructive attack, but without the desired success, for in March, 1887, Mr. S. D.

---

* Report of Prof. C. V. Riley, Entomologist of the Department of Agriculture, U. S. A., for 1886, pub. 1887, Washington (see, for *I. purchasi*, pp. 466—492, and plates). 'Insects noxious to Agriculture, &c., in New Zealand. The Scale Insects *Coccididæ*,' 1887, by W. M. Maskell, F.R.M.S., Wellington, N.Z.

† See Report by Mr. Roland Trimen, Curator of the S. African Mus., on the insect of the family Coccidæ, commonly known as the "Australian Bug." Government notice (Blue Book), No. 113, 1877.

Bairstow, of Port Elizabeth, President of the East Province Naturalists' Society, wrote me : — " The Australian Bug seems to be extending operations in Bloemfontein and higher up country." This observation, together with the foregoing, shows a spread over a length of 680 miles—that is, from Cape Town to Bloemfontein —during the fourteen years which then had passed since first observation of the pest in the Colony, and a glance at the map of South Africa will show the vast extent of area of the Eastern division in which the pest had then naturalised itself. Where it came from does not appear to be proved, but there does not appear room for doubt that the attack was set on foot by imported specimens, and that it rapidly became naturalised.

The Bug appears to attack such a great variety of trees, bushes, &c., that it may be well described as a general pest. Oranges, or plants of the *Citrus* tribe, are especially infested by it. Vine and fig are also mentioned specially as injured by it, and more generally deciduous fruit trees, ornamental shrubs, and garden plants, the list ranging down to strawberry plants.

AUSTRALIAN BUG.

FIG. 28.—Cluster of female Bugs, photographed from life at Adelaide, South Australia, by Frazer S. Crawford, Esq.

The figs. given at p. 69 and above, from S. African, S. Australian, and N. American specimens, show the similarity of the appearance of the infested twigs in different countries. These show the female scales in the groups in which they are to be found on twigs or leafage.

The adult females which were sent me from Port Elizabeth, with the white-striped egg-bag attached, were about a quarter of an inch long, and of the shape figured magnified on the left hand of figure on p. 69,— that is, somewhat tortoise-shaped, and arched up from each side and each end. The hinder part of the true abdomen of the " Bug " is hidden by the fore part of the egg-bag, and is tilted up by the vast number of eggs which gradually accumulate beneath. The colour of the insect is of some shade of orange or salmon, for the most part covered on the upper side, and partially on the under side, by a whitish mealy-looking coat. When magnified this appearance is shown to be formed of little rough patches of a white cotton-like or waxy secretion, which are largest and thickest towards the fore part of the insect, and are mixed with a sprinkling of black hairs. These hairs are set much more thickly at the edges, and form almost a fringe at the hinder part, to which the white longitudinally striped egg-bag is appended.

Fig. 29.—Female of *Icerya purchasi ;* under side and antenna (much magnified.)

Whether this sac is easily separable when fresh I do not know, but, after soaking some time in spirits of wine, I found it could be easily detached, and the insect attached was found to be a soft, thick, fleshy, oval mass, the place of the thorax or fore body being shown above by three slightly raised, convex, transverse ridges, each bearing a slight knob or elevation in the middle. The fore edge of the insect is thickened and slightly scalloped, and with a few ridges running from the edge to the foremost ridge. Beneath it is furnished with three pairs of legs, a pair of horns or antennæ (see fig. 29), and a sucker placed between the two foremost pairs of legs (all black or pitchy). The antennæ or horns did not appear to me to be of more than ten joints, of the same width throughout, excepting the lowest joint, which is

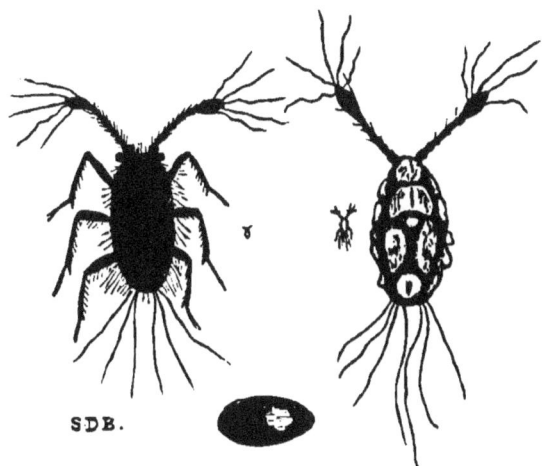

AUSTRALIAN BUG.

FIG. 30.—Egg mag., larvæ mag. and nat. size; back of one larva showing cottony patches.* After figs. by S. D. Bairstow.

somewhat wider than the others: it was not clear whether the apparently long joint immediately succeeding was of two joints, or of one slightly marked across in the centre; but as the specimens examined had been

---

* Accompanying Mr. Bairstow's sketches of the larva were notes of his daily, or almost daily, observations of the early history of the " Bug " from hatching onwards, during a period of two months, extending from the latter part of January to the end of March,—the main points of which I have already published in my pamphlet on *Icerya purchasi.*

long in spirit, I have no doubt that they were really eleven, jointed like those described by MM. Signoret, Maskell, Comstock, and other observers.

The egg-sac is white, formed of minute threads exuded by the insect, and is striped from the line of its attachment to the body, to the hinder extremity or sides, by about fifteen parallel, round-topped ridges, having deep hollows between. In the case of some of the sacs which I examined, the central longitudinal ridge was narrowest, even to being half the width only of the others.

The general appearance of the female is well described by the name of " Cottony Cushion Scale," used in California, or also the name of " Ribbed Scale." Within the sac lie a multitude of oval salmon-coloured eggs, as many, it is stated, as from 200 upwards.

In Prof. Trimen's Report he states that the young hatch gradually from the eggs deposited in the cottony nidus, but appear only to leave it by degrees, till at length all have departed, and the empty skin of the dead mother alone remains behind.

Mr. Bairstow also remarked on this head : — " The Bugs do not all hatch at once. I do not remark any sudden exit or uniformity and spontaneousness in clearance. Several days are occupied in effecting a total riddance from the oviparous mother." And he further observed of the young Bugs, that "when hatched and emerging from the maternal nidus the spider-like insects are extremely active for about thirty-six hours; then they choose a spot for settlement and remain stationary."

The two figures of larvæ are taken from a series of slight pen-and-ink sketches made from life by Mr. Bairstow to illustrate the changes of appearance of the specimens under observation, the first showing the general appearance in an early stage of development, the second showing the patchy appearance of the fine growth of the flocculent covering.

From my own examination of the larva in the first

stage (figured p. 73), as seen after being in a preservative fluid for some time, it was of a reddish tint, with black legs and antennæ and black eyes, and was furnished at the tip of the abdomen with six long fine hairs. The horns at this stage appear to me to be formed of five joints and a club. The lowest joint broad and short, about half the length and twice the width of the succeeding joint, and broadest at the farthest end from the head ; the following four joints are almost cylindrical, the second of these being longer than the first and slightly contracted at the centre : a very few long scattered hairs were observable on the joints of the horns.

Prof. Trimen notes that when the Bug has reached about one-sixth of an inch in length it begins to secrete the snow-white, waxy, but cotton-like, matter, which presently forms a nest beneath the mother insect for the salmon-coloured eggs. "For some time after the white secretion" has begun to grow the *Dorthesia* remains tolerably active, continuing to move about, and change its feeding-ground on "the plant; but gradually, as the ova develop and the cottony secretion proportionately enlarges, its power of motion seems to decrease, and at length it remains firmly anchored to one spot by its sucker"; and as time goes on the newly-hatched young are to be found, which leave the cottony nest beneath the dead mother, and, being gifted with much greater powers of locomotion at this stage than later on, seek actively for a suitable place where they may settle down to feed (see Prof. Trimen's Report).

The observations of Mr. Bairstow and Prof. Trimen, above quoted, taken together, give a large part of the life-history that is needed for practical service. We have observations of the eggs hatching in the white deposit, and the little Buglets coming out and spreading actively from under the dead skin of the mother Bug; also of this activity continuing more or less from about the beginning of February until at least the 21st of March : we have further the observations of the white secretion under the Bug beginning when it is about the

sixth of an inch long : and also we have observations
of the gradually settling down into stationary condition

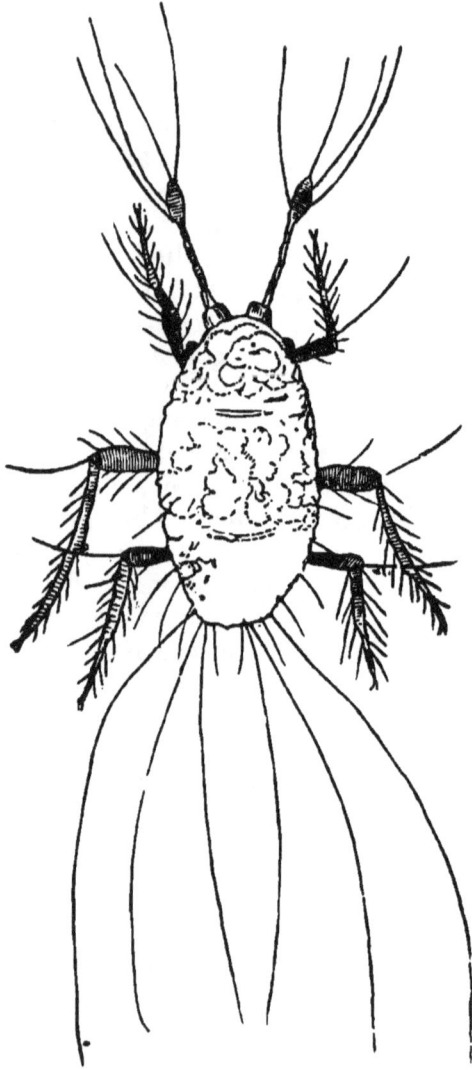

ICERYA PURCHASI.   (S. Australia.)
FIG. 31.—Larva, enormously magnified; nat. size about 1-16th in.

of the female Bug, as the amount of white waxy deposit increases until she becomes a mere dead husk covering

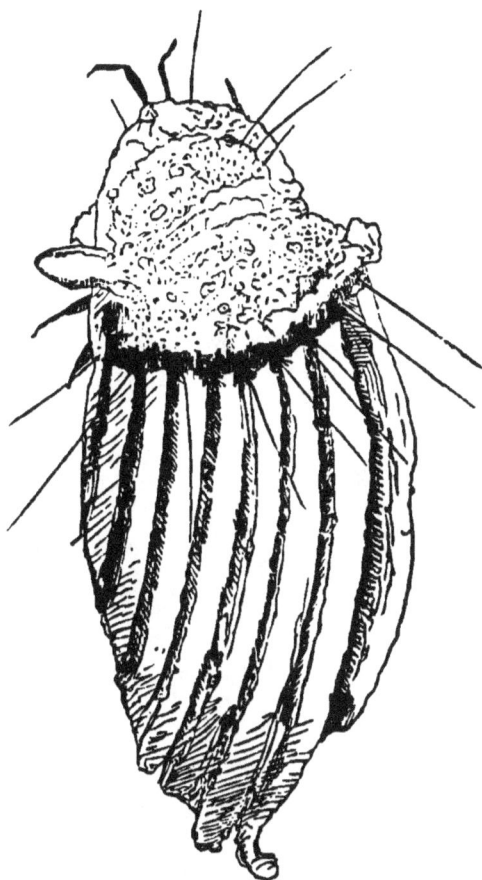

FIG. 32.—*Icerya purchasi* (S. Australia). Adult female with egg-bag, greatly magnified.

the eggs and hatching young. The whole process extends over many weeks, and gives ample opportunity for immense damage to be caused by the bugs.

Whilst my previous notice of Australian Bug was passing through press I was favoured by Mr. Frazer S.

Crawford,* of Adelaide, S. Australia, who for some years
has devoted special attention to the habits of this pest,
with the two preceding sketches, giving very greatly
magnified representations of the larva and adult
female of the *I. purchasi* from photographs taken by
himself.

Mr. Crawford's figure (see page 77) is of especial
interest, from showing the striated nature of the egg-
sac, and the long glassy filaments, which are characteristic distinctions of the adult female of *I. purchasi*.

I am not aware whether up to the present date the
male insect has been observed with identification in
S. Africa, and therefore I subjoin a description abridged
from that given by Prof. Riley, and taken by him from
numerous specimens, both mounted and living, of the
Icerya purchasi Maskell, and likewise a copy of Prof.
Riley's figure.†

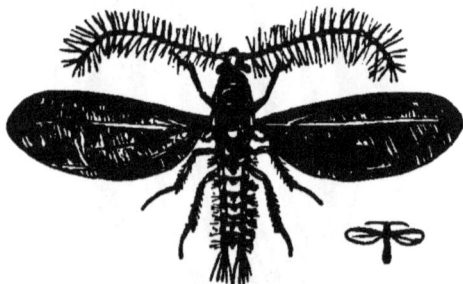

FIG. 83.—*Icerya purchasi*, male insect, nat. size and magnified.

Prof. Riley states that "the adult male is a trifle over

* Government Inspector under the Vine, Fruit, and Vegetables Protection Act, and Lecturer on Economic Entomology, &c.

† For above see paper, noted p. 70, on *I. purchasi*, by Prof. Riley, in his
Report as U. S. Entomologist, published by the Commissioner of Agriculture of the United States of America, and figure of the male insect
in the plates of illustration to the same; and further, I must add that,
once again in this re-publication of my pamphlet, I desire to offer my
thanks to Prof. Riley for his kind courtesy in permitting me to see his
proof-sheets before publication and to benefit by the above observation.
Those who desire to study the subject *in extenso* cannot do better than
avail themselves of the immense amount of practical and scientific
information embodied in his paper above quoted.

3 mm. in length " [that is, over the eighth of an English inch in length —E. A. O.], " and has an average wing-expanse of 7·5 mm. The general colour is orange-red." The thorax is much marked with black; some of the spiracles are black also. " The legs are also nearly black, and quite thickly furnished with short hairs. The wings are smoky black, and are covered with rounded wavy elevations, making a reticulate surface. The costa is thick and brown above the subcostal vein, which reaches costa at a trifle more than four-fifths the length of the wing. · The only other vein (the median) is given off at about one-sixth of the length of the wing, and extends out into the disk a little more than one-half the wing-length. There are in addition two white lines, one extending" . . . to the tip of the wing, the other curving to a point some distance below the tip. " The abdomen is slightly hairy, . . . and is furnished at tip with two strong projections, each of which bears at tip four long hairs and a few shorter ones. When the insect is at rest the wings lie flat on the back." The head above is triangular; the antennæ are light brown in colour, and are composed of ten joints, of which the first is almost globular, the second somewhat longer, and the third nearly twice as long as the first, and the remaining seven joints are of about the same length as the third, "and grow successively a little more slender."

Measures of Prevention and Remedy.

The following observations and recipes are given as not only referring to applications for destruction of Australian Bug, but for reference with regard to many other insect attacks which may be much checked by soft-soap washes :—

Washes.

Looking at the impossibility of clearing more than a very small proportion of the pest by hand-picking (as obviously *much* of it is out of reach, and likewise that most of it which may be in reach, excepting the large females, is too small to be hand-picked) ; also, looking at the great difficulty, in the case of partially clearing trees by shaking off the pest, of making sure that a quantity does not remain on the ground to creep up the trees again, it would appear that what is required is some mixture to destroy the pest on the infested tree. Something is needed—1st, which will *not* hurt the tree or plant ; 2nd, which *will* hurt the " Bug," or render it harmless to us whatever stage it may be in ; and 3rd, this mixture needs to be something that *can* be applied effectually with reasonable ease and at small cost. In the early days of attack soft-soap wash is alluded to as a thing found useful in one locality ; since then its serviceableness has been brought forward elsewhere in Cape Colony, and most strongly as of use in California, and looking at the great success of soft-soap washes now used on such a large scale for destroying Aphides (no distant relations of these " Bugs ") in England, it appears well worth while to give one or two of the recipes for keeping down the pest in California ; and likewise some of the methods of preparing the mixtures of soft-soap and mineral oil for safe and convenient use, which have been worked out since Prof. Trimen suggested something of this nature might probably be of use.

If a minute's thought is given to the subject it will be seen that the soft- or whale-oil soap cannot fail to be beneficial by sticking on the surface of the Bugs, and choking their breathing-pores, and likewise by soaking under the egg-bags of the females and destroying both the young which are on the point of escaping, as well as those which are exposed outside. It would also be to a certain extent a preventive to the infestation being blown about the country by the wind, a matter which Mr. Bairstow especially notes as one method of spread.

One of the remedies recommended by Mr. Matthew

Cooke for destruction of this scale-insect in California*
is a wash of whale-oil, or soft-soap, sulphur, and
tobacco, in the proportion of one pound of the soap
to a third of a pound of sulphur, the sulphur to be
boiled in water for ten or fifteen minutes, and the soap
then added, and to each gallon of this mixture one
gallon of tobacco water to be added of the strength noted
below.† The mixture to be applied at a temperature of
130° Fahr.

In the above mixture no mention is made regarding
method of dissolving the sulphur, and the following
recipe for a soft-soap wash with the sulphur in solution
might prove serviceable:—In order to make sulphur
combine with whatever liquid may be used, the sulphur
should be boiled with an alkali, and the recipe has been
recommended:—One pound of flour of sulphur and two
pounds of fresh lime boiled together in four gallons of
water: or, to save the trouble of boiling, sulphuret of
lime may be purchased and used thus: of this sulphuret
take four ounces, soft-soap two ounces, to each gallon
of hot water; the soap and sulphuret to be well mixed
before the addition of the water, which is to be gradually
poured on, the mixture being stirred during the time,
when a uniform fluid will be obtained without sediment,
which may be used when cool enough to bear the hand,
and has been found to destroy insect pests effectually
and quickly. This may be used as a syringing, or a dip
for infested shoots, or well rubbed with a brush into
infested bark. The mixture, like other soft-soap washes,
may be thrown when requisite to a height of several
yards by large garden-engines, such as are used in
Hop-fields in England. If it is needed higher, and
water and apparatus are attainable, trees of even
considerable height may be "washed" by the help of a

* See 'Injurious Insects of the Orchard,' &c., by Matthew Cooke (late
Chief Executive Horticultural Officer of California), pp. 165—167, with
account of "Cottony Cushion Scale," and references to recipes for
applications to destroy the scale, in same work.

† Boil 30 pounds of tobacco leaves in 30 gallons of water.

G

fire-engine.   I have had this done in England under
special circumstances, with great success.

The following note by Mr. W. G. Klee, State Inspector
of Fruit Pests in California, regards application of
various forms of soft-soap wash for the extermination
of the Australian Bug, or "Cottony Cushion Scale," as
it is well named in California, on small evergreen trees,
or on deciduous trees when out of leaf or lopped back
to the main trunk or branches. [It will be observed that
the ingredients of the wash that are given in full detail
are especially directed to be *boiled*.   Probably much
danger and damage would be spared if attention was
always directed to the point that *soft-soap washes should
be raised to boiling-point in the process of mixing.*—ED.]
Mr. Klee states :—"For all deciduous trees . . . we
recommend one-fourth of a pound of concentrated lye,
one-fourth of a pound of whale-oil soap, to one gallon
of water.   Before treating the tree, cut off the tops down
to the main branches and burn them.

" For evergreens the summer wash recommended last
summer is useful, and will not hurt healthy foliage :
dissolve 30 pounds whale-oil soap (80 per cent. soap at
the most costing 5 cents per pound) in 60 gallons of
water by heating the whole thoroughly.   Boil 3 pounds
of lye (American concentrated lye is what we have used)
with 6 pounds of sulphur and a couple of gallons of
water.   When thoroughly dissolved it is a dark brown
liquid (chemically sulphide of soda).   Mix the two,
the soap and the sulphide of soda, well, and allow
them to boil for about half an hour ; then add about
90 gallons of water to the mixture, and it is ready for
use.

" Apply it warm, at about 130° Fahr., by means of a
spray-pump.   Used warm its effect is better, and less
material is required than when cold.   It must, however,
be remembered that the minute scales are especially
numerous on the under side of leaves.   This fact makes
the extermination on a large tree in full foliage almost
impossible.   Only small trees may be successfully treated

in this way. Large trees must be either deprived of their foliage or cut down to a few limbs.

"Neither of these methods can be safely applied on tender trees during a season when sharp frost may be looked for. A spraying should, however, be done, as it will check their spread most effectually.

"*Too great pains cannot be taken in removing infested limbs,* * *as the insect spreads often in this way. A canvas should be spread under the trees so that none of the insects can escape.* When the tree has been treated spread hot ashes around its base, and apply tight-fitting bands smeared with a greasy substance around the trunk to prevent any insects reascending."—W. G. KLEE, Inspector of Fruit Trees.†

Washes of Soft-soap in combination with Petroleum, Paraffin, or other Mineral Oils.

In the Report on Australian Bug, prepared by Prof. R. Trimen, he mentions that "it might be worth while to try one of the antidotes used against the *Phylloxera* in France, *viz.*, petroleum and water," &c.; and since the date of the Report the serviceableness of mineral oils as insecticides, when so *combined* with soft-soap and water that they may be diluted further as may be needed for use *without risk of the oil and water separating again*, has been strongly brought forward under the direction of the Department of Agriculture of the United States, and reported on at length by Prof. Riley.

The U. S. A. plan is to add one gallon of water, in which a quarter of a pound of soft-soap (or any other coarse soap preferred) has been well dissolved, boiling or hot, to two gallons of petroleum or other mineral oil.

* The point of spread of the pest being likely to be encouraged, rather than checked, by infested boughs being removed without due care as to what becomes of the dislodged and shaken-off insects, is so important that I have given it in italics.—ED.

† Bulletin No. 4 of State Board of Horticulture of California. Winter washes recommended by the State Inspector of Fruit Pests. Sacramento, State Office, 1887.

The mixture is then churned, as it were, together by
means of a spray-nozzled syringe, or double-action pump,
for ten minutes, by means of which the oil, soap, and
water are so thoroughly combined that the mixture settles
down into a cream-like consistency, and does not, if the
operation has been properly performed, separate again.
This is used diluted with some three or four times its
bulk of water for a watering; if required for a wash, at
least nine times its bulk is needed,—that is, three gallons
of "Emulsion," as it is termed, make thirty gallons of
wash.   Warning is given that care must be taken with
each new crop to ascertain the strength that can be
borne by the leafage : this of course varies with the age
of the leaves, as well as the nature of the crop.

In my own experiments with this mixture I increased
the quantity of soft-soap, and for Hop-plants I should
consider it would be desirable to *double* the proportion of
soft-soap and *lessen* that of the paraffin to at least a sixth.

An addition of some amount of paraffin to soft-soap
wash has been shown to be serviceable by the experiments
of Mr. Ward at Stoke Edith in 1883 and the following
season.   The proportions used by him for large quantities
are 12 pounds of soft-soap and half a gallon of paraffin
to 100 gallons of hot water, the mixture stirred well
together and used when cool ; the nearer boiling that
the water is used the better the paraffin mixes.   This
wash is found to be very effective in killing the Aphides
without injuring the plant or the burr.

For low shrubs or plants to which application could
be made by means of a watering-can, the mixture of
which the details of preparation and convenient method
of storing are given as follows, would probably be found
serviceable :—

"To eight parts of soft water add one part of black
(soft) soap, and boil briskly for a few minutes until the
soap is thoroughly dissolved.   While boiling add paraffin,
or any similar mineral oil, and boil for a minute or two
longer, when the whole will be thoroughly amalgamated,*

* For field use the immediate application would save all need of

and, if bottled and securely corked while warm, it will remain so, and be fit for use at any time when required. The strength of the solution of course depends on the amount of mineral oil in it, and it can be easily reduced to the proper power by mixing it with soft water as it is wanted for use."

Mr. Malcolm Dunn gave me the following notes as to the method he found most convenient for mixing the application :—" In practice I boil the proper proportions of soap and water together, and when ready I fill this into ordinary wine-bottles, which have been placed in boiling water. The bottles are about half-filled with the lye, and then the paraffin is poured into them. *two gills* being put into each bottle. The bottles are then filled up with the boiling lye, corked at once, and stored away for use.

" When required for use a bottle of the mixture is poured into a four-gallon watering-pot, which is filled up with soft water, and is ready for use, at a strength of one wine-glass of paraffin (*half a gill*) to one gallon of water."

Mr. Dunn further notes that the important point is the proportion of the soap and water :—"*Eight parts water and one part soft-soap thoroughly amalgamated* form the lye which *takes* mineral oil, and thoroughly amalgamates with whatever proportion of this may be added,—that is to say, the paraffin may be put into the boiling soap and water in any quantity, and the whole will mix together of an equal strength throughout. Heat helps much in quickly producing thorough amalgamation of all the ingredients, and hence I have stated that they should be mixed in a *boiling state*.

" Few plants in a *green state* will stand a strength of four wine-glasses (two gills) *to the gallon*, but at the same time *it is not necessary to use it so strong for even Scale-insects*, the most difficult to kill of all ordinary plant-pests.

storing. For garden use the arrangement of bottling saves much risk from careless workers, as the exact amount to be used can be given out.

"One wine-glass full of paraffin to a gallon of water is strong enough to kill Aphides, and such soft insects ; two wine-glasses for Thrips, and three wine-glasses for Scale is our ' regulation' strength. The tender young fronds of ferns and the *young green growths of most plants will not be safe if over one wine-glass to the gallon is used.*" *

The following note regarding spread of Australian Bug during the year 1886, and means considered to be useful in checking its increase, was forwarded me by favour of Mr. F. von Schade, of Wynberg :—" The Australian Bug (*Dorthesia*) has made its appearance in the village of Oudtshoorn, and we advise the property-holders to exert much vigilance in exterminating it at·once. Putrid blood has proved a good exterminator of the Bug. The stems and branches of trees must be painted with the blood, the smell of which attracts numerous insects which devour the Bug. Ostrich droppings boiled in water and the solution syringed on the higher branches of trees has also been found very effective. Then there is the solution made of tobacco and whale-soap for washing and syringing."—' Wynberg Times,' July 31st, 1886.

[If the blood could be applied to the stems and branches of the trees as a painting, there would not be difficulty in applying a good painting or *scrubbing* with a thick soft-soap solution, which would probably have an excellent effect.—ED.]

In regard to methods of application one great difficulty is how to throw the fluids high enough to reach the upper boughs and foliage of moderate-sized trees. Of this Prof. Comstock says that the difficulty is best met by using some kind of force-pump, by which mixtures can be sprayed on the infested plants. The pump he recommends is formed of two brass tubes, one working telescopically within the other ; a hose is fastened to one

* ' Eighth Report of Observations of Injurious Insects,' 1884, published 1885. By E. A. Ormerod. Simpkin, Marshall & Co., London, England.

end, and a rose can be attached to the other ; an arrangement of valves allows water to pass into the pump through the hose, but will not allow it to return. Thus, when the smaller tube is pulled out the pump is filled to its greatest capacity; by pushing this tube back the water can be ejected with considerable force through the rose in a fine spray. By using a nozzle with a single opening a stream can be thrown to a greater distance. In this way the topmost leaves of any orchard tree can be reached. In applying liquids on a large scale, as upon extensive orchards, the work can be done rapidly by placing the mixture in a barrel upon a waggon, and pumping directly from this barrel. It is noted that from the great difficulty of wetting every part of. the tree by a single application, that probably several will be necessary.*

Destruction by Hand-picking and shaking down the Bug from infested Trees.

Prof. Trimen states that he regards it as of "the first importance to destroy all the larger specimens, for from these legions of young are perpetually proceeding, and the effectual destruction of a single gravid female means that of at least 150 or 200 young ones." He mentions that he has found "that the larger specimens may often be detached by shaking a plant, or, in the case of trees, striking the branches smartly with a stick. When this is done a cloth, or sheets of paper, should be spread under the shaken or beaten branches to catch the insects as they drop, otherwise some of them will break on striking the ground and the eggs or young escape." He further advises, in the same Report, "that all the insects collected together should be burnt forthwith, as they resist immersion in water for a long time, and the eggs or minute young in the mass of white secretion are unaffected by it. Crushing the old ones is also only

* 'Report of the Entomologist of the United States Department of Agriculture for the year 1880,' By H. Comstock. Washington, 1881.

partly effectual, many of the enclosed young escaping
the pressure unhurt."*

Mr. S. D. Bairstow also draws attention to the benefit
of destroying the female, and the ease with which the
young may be shaken from the trees.

As these young Bugs are so active and fall off so readily
it would appear very desirable, where boughs have been
lopped or infested trees felled, that these boughs or trees
should be burnt (or charred on the surface) at once, and
on the spot, or else, as is pointed out in the Report of the
Inspector of Fruit Trees in California, published in the
year 1887, the removal of the boughs may in itself be
a means of spreading the pest.

Tarred bands, or bands of any sticky composition,
smeared round the lower part of the stems of fruit or
timber trees, would effectually stop traffic of the "Bug"
up the trunks so long as the bands remained moist and
sticky ; but, if the thing be possible, some more secure
method of gathering the fallen, active, young Bugs, or
preventing their ranging off to some of the low-growing
plants near, than what has been named seems needed.

In U. S. A. practice the plan of beating injurious
insects down on to cloths treated with some fluid or
mixture which will temporarily paralyse the grubs or
insects as they fall on to it, or possibly kill them out-
right, has been recommended, and in the present case it
appears quite admisssible that the cloths recommended
to be placed under the trees to be beaten should be so
prepared beforehand. There are many mixtures of
petroleum or other mineral oils which would probably
answer the purposes. The fact of the oil soon separating
from water would not matter in this case, and the cloths
might be dipped in a mere mixture of the petroleum and
water, and used wet, or they might be drenched over
(when laid down) with soft-soap and petroleum wash,
which would presumably prevent any of these little
creatures straying away ; or a good swilling on to the

---

* 'Report on Australian Bug,' by Prof. R. Trimen, previously quoted.

ground of soft-soap wash would be a great preventive of wandering.

In England, for prevention of wandering from a given point, it is sometimes found useful to circumscribe a small area with a line of wet tar, and where there were only the droppings from a few trees or the infestation in a limited spot to be temporarily dealt with, it might save all trouble to run a little furrow (just to save waste in application), and to pour some tar along it, renewing it for a day or two if necessary ; but in whatever way it is managed, it is obvious, from the remark of the Inspector of Fruit Pests of California, quoted at p. 83, that the point of the spread of the attack from the pest being dispersed in removing the infected trees requires much consideration.

On Aug. 21st, 1886, Mr. Bairstow wrote :—" I notice that the large female attacks the black-wood roots most fiercely in the winter time.   Just now " [winter in Cape Colony—ED.] " in St. George's Park the ground in some parts is simply alive—*snowy*—with them."   At this period a little care and attention must prove amazingly beneficial.

How far mechanical measures can be brought to bear on such a state of things as that above described can only be certainly known by trial, but it occurs whether something might not be done towards gathering a large amount of the pests off the grass by running a machine over it, made on the principle of a lawn-mowing machine, with brushes instead of cutters.   It would on the face of the thing appear likely that, by a little arrangement to allow of the brushes just catching on the edge of the box, so as to free themselves of the Bugs sticking on to them, much might be cleared from the ground and swept up into the box and destroyed.   If all other measures failed, good hearty sweeping of the grass with brooms or brushes frequently dipped in soft-soap solution would clear an appreciable amount, and would at least be better than leaving the creatures to be dispersed as chance might cause.

When the trees, or groves of trees, are infested, it is

manifest that it is only by the most wholesale or broad
scale measures that anything can be done to check
attack, but (looking at the great variety of plants mentioned as liable to be infested by this pest from the
quantities creeping in the grass upwards) it is very plain
that there is no hope of stopping the spread of the pest
by the destruction of only a *portion of its haunts*, such
as fruit or timber trees, and that general measures are
greatly needed, and a careful watch to prevent attack
getting hold.

Amongst these the danger of transmission should in
every way be guarded against ; the processes of removal
of parts of trees which have been felled to get rid of
the Bug cannot be too often pointed out, as being
exceedingly likely to cause carriage also of the pest,
and likewise all plants received from doubtful localities
should be carefully investigated ; and no one with any
thought for the welfare of his neighbours should allow
the smallest plant with the " Bug " on it to be carried
from his grounds.

But with regard to applications that may be serviceable
for use against the Australian Bug (the Cottony Cushion-
Scale of North America), it would be equally pre-
sumptuous and unnecessary at this date to offer any
special suggestions on this subject, as in the Report of
the Commissioner of Agriculture of the United States,
before mentioned, it will be found in the observations
tendered by Prof. Riley, from Mr. D. W. Coquillett, and
likewise from Mr. Albert Koebele, of Alameda, California,
that these points are minutely dealt with.

In these observations are given as to effects, good or
bad, of caustic potash and caustic soda, hard soap, soft
soap, kerosene emulsions, tobacco, tobacco-soap, sheep-
dip, vinegar and Paris-green, bisulphide of carbon, resin-
soap, whale-oil, &c. ; and, besides methods of and
appliances for throwing the washes, and methods of
mixing or preparing the same, notes are given of little
less than 153 experiments tried by Mr. Albert Koebele,
with mention of material used, proportion of water
added, and the results of the application.

Insect Enemies.

The carnivorous larva or maggot of a species of *Chrysopa* or Lace-winged Fly, or "Golden Eye," and also the grubs of a Coccinellid or Ladybird, have been observed by Mr. Bairstow to do much good by destroying the young Australian Bugs, just at hatching time, within the sac of the female.

Of these Mr. Bairstow says :—" The *Coccinella* is by far our best friend. It is proving a perfect god-send in destroying the perfected young in nidus of the female 'Bug.' The larva buries itself in the gravid female and completely destroys her progeny, the dead carcase falling to the ground ; and it eats the ' Bug ' not only when it is young, but when it (the *Coccinella*) has developed to beetle condition. I have taken as many as five or six young Bugs out of the inside of one of these *Coccinellæ* or Ladybird Beetles. The changes from grub to beetle are rapidly passed through, as with other *Coccinellidæ*."

Its efficacy cannot be over-estimated, and an importation of the *Coccinellæ* to infested regions would be certain to be of service.—S. D. B.

This species of South African Coccinellid is of the size and shape figured, and may be generally described as black, with a blood-red spot in the centre at the base of the wing-cases, and clothed with thick short down above ; the under side and legs reddish, and also downy.

As this "Ladybird" does not appear to have been previously described, I placed it in the hands of Mr. Oliver E. Janson, of London, England, who was good enough to examine it for me ; and on it proving to be a species as yet undescribed of the genus *Rodolia*, it has appeared desirable to

Rodolia iceryæ, n. sp.

mark it by a specific name pointing to its serviceable habits of destruction of the *Icerya*—as the *Rodolia iceryæ*,

Janson, n. sp. I append Mr. Janson's technical description,* and also give the following more general note of appearance with which he favoured me :—

"Of our English *Coccinellidæ* the *Rodolia* most nearly resembles *Chilocorus bipustulatus :* it is about the same size as the common Two-spot Ladybird (*Coccinella bipunctata*), but is of a more convex and hemispherical form ; the thorax is much shorter, and has the sides narrow, rounded, and bent down ; the head is short, vertical, and concealed beneath the thorax ; the legs are short, and flattened with the tibiæ angulated and grooved for the reception of the tarsi ; it is black above, with a peculiar dusty or powdered appearance produced by the fine short grey pubescence with which it is covered, and has a large, conspicuous blood-red spot in the centre at the base of the elytra ; the underside and legs are pale rusty red."—O. E. J.

A slight sketch of the maggot sent by Mr. Bairstow showed it to have the somewhat elongate form common to larvæ of this family, three pairs of claw-legs and jaws (which it uses to good purposes), and that the sides of the segments were furnished with pencils of hairs.

The figure of the pupa- or chrysalis-case represented this stage as passed in the typical manner of this family, namely, that after the larva has become full-grown it

* "*Rodolia iceryæ*, n. sp.—Almost hemispherical, a little longer than broad, and slightly narrowed behind ; above very finely and closely punctured, and rather densely clothed with fine grey pubescence ; shining black, with a large semicircular blood-red spot at the base of the elytra, enclosing the scutellum. Head flattened ; inner margin of the eyes straight ; antennæ, palpi, and labrum, red. Thorax produced and rounded posteriorly, truncate in front of the scutellum, strongly produced and rounded at the sides, the lateral margin slightly reflexed, anterior margin narrowly testaceous. Scutellum elongate-triangular, the apex acute. Elytra impressed on each side of the scutellum, the humeral callus very prominent, humeral angles somewhat produced anteriorly, rounded, and slightly elevated. Under side and legs pale red, strongly punctured, and with fine pubescence ; epipleuræ strongly concave, black ; tibiæ strongly emarginate for the reception of the tarsi, the outer edge strongly but obtusely angulated and fringed with long grey hairs. Length 4—5 millim."—'Notes on the Australian Bug in South Africa,' p. 30.

fastens itself by the end of its tail to a leaf or some other point of attachment, and then rolls off its maggot-skin up to the end of the body, and waits thus affixed till the pupal changes have been completed, and the Ladybird emerges from the pupa or chrysalis.

Another of the enemies of the Australian Bug by which the increase of this pest in S. Africa is materially checked is a species of *Chrysopa* or " Golden Eye," one of the *Hemerobiidæ* or " Lace-wings," a family of which the grubs or larvæ are sometimes known, from one large item of their food, as Aphis Lions. Of these grubs Mr. Bairstow says :—" I do not wish it to be understood that this singular larva preys solely upon *Dorthesia* " (Australian Bug.—E. A. O.). . . . . . But that the larva

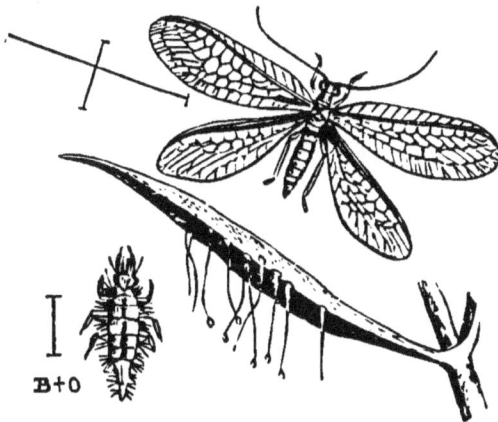

FIG. 31.—*Chrysopa (? iceryæ,* n. sp.). Insect and larva, magnified, with lines showing nat. size. (Sketch showing appearance of stalked eggs of *Hemerobiidæ.*

decidedly prefers *Dorthesia*, if it can be obtained, I rest assured, both from out-of-door observations and practical experiments. As the insect appears to be as yet undescribed, I have suggested that the specific name of *iceryæ* should be bestowed on it (provisionally at least) as well as on the *Rodolia*, with reference to the special article of its food. In common with other species of the

Hemerobiidæ or Lace-wings the perfect insect flies in the
daytime, but is not readily disturbed when at rest. It is
short-lived."

"The imago is of the size and shape figured, with
four iridescent azure and pink tinted transparent wings,
brownish green body, and yellow head and thorax. Eyes
deep purple, with a rusty tinge, and encircled with red.
Antennæ long and slender. Wing-expanse about seven-
eighths of an inch. Length of body about a quarter of
an inch."

The larva or grub is of the shape copied from Mr.
Bairstow's sketch (see figure, with the natural size
accompanying),. and of a dirty brown colour above, and
whitish below (for full description see note) ; and has the
remarkable habit, in common with others of its kind, of
piling a covering of scraps on its own back.*

Mr. Bairstow thus notes the method of operation of
the grub :—"Travelling up and down a branch, he at
last approached a good fat specimen of *Dorthesia*, and
began dragging with his mandibles pieces of the woolly
nidus, which he carefully arranged, and, throwing his
head backward, steadily deposited the fragments on his
body until it was quite covered. This I found was afterwards utilised in metamorphosis for a domicile to protect
it in chrysalis state, and, being coated inside with some
gummy secretion, made. a hard exterior and capital
fortress ; but in wrenching away the white nest from the
female bug, he was demolishing the only protection for

* DESCRIPTION OF LARVA OF *Chrysopa* (? *iceryæ*, n. sp.).—Length ¼ inch.
Dirty brown on back, darkest where the woolly deposit is situated.
Beneath : semitransparent dirty grey, with deep brown divisional and
segmental markings. A longitudinal centre band forming grey irregularly-
shaped squares of varied dimensions centred on each, with dark brown
semitransparent spot and lateral marks of grey. Under prothorax and
thorax external organs are set off with a pale salmon-pink colour, very
variable in different specimens. Tarsal tips and anus black. The lateral
tubercles on each segment are setiferous and very conspicuous 1st, 2nd,
and 3rd being most prominent. First, dirty white, edged with black, and
setæ corresponding ; others dull white at base, and paler setæ. Ocelli
black, also longitudinal markings or laminæ reaching from near base of
mandibles to second pair of tubercles, black and conspicuous. Jaws about
one-sixth length of body ; palpi and antennæ prominent.—S. D. B.

the eggs and young buglets sheltered within. Having at last pulled away enough to expose the residents, he seized on them one by one, and, after sucking all vitality out, flung away the empty skin."

For further observation ten or twelve of these "Aphis Lions" were placed with six gravid female "Bugs," one of which was opened by a cut across the white waxy egg-nest, thus exposing the eggs and young within, which were reckoned by Mr. Bairstow as amounting to as many as five hundred, if all hatched. At the end of the first day the whole collection in the opened female had been destroyed by the voracious little Aphis Lions ; they then attacked the other female Bugs, and at the end of five days scarcely a bugling survived.

The observer further remarks that he has noticed "scores of times" that well-developed females which he saw on a branch on one afternoon would next morning show only as broken egg-bags, empty and torn to shreds, and, as they could not have all hatched and got away, it appeared plain there was something at work "struggling to assist in keeping a proper balance, and this, after search, was found in the shape of a *Hemerobius* grub, a small larva with big jaws, demolishing *Dorthesia* in scores."

Mr. Bairstow remarks that the voracious larva is much assisted in catching its prey by the structure which enables it to use its long jaws in various directions, and thus grasp the eggs as well as capture the young bugs ; also that it is readily detected in its native haunts, either as a grub or pupa, by the powdery mass of covering which it assumes, and which when pilfered from the bug gives it a completely snow-flake appearance ; or when at rest it might be passed over as a small mass of spider's web.

The precise description of the egg has not been given, but it is the nature of the *Hemerobiidæ*, to which family this Golden Eye belongs, for the female to discharge a small quantity of sticky matter in the process of laying each egg. This draws out in the operation into a long

fine thread, at the free extremity of which the egg is
borne very much like the head of a pin on its stem. The
sketch of eggs added to those of the larva and perfect
insect of this Golden Eye merely conveys an idea of the
general method of egg-deposit of this family.

Yet another insect aider in keeping down what has
not been ill termed the "Scourge of S. Africa" may
very likely be introduced by importing from S. Australia
the dipterous parasite first observed by Mr. Frazer S.
Crawford, in his garden, at Adelaide.

In the course of correspondence with Mr. Frazer
Crawford, of Adelaide (Government Inspector under the
Vine, Fruit and Vegetable Protection Act, and Lecturer
on Economic Entomology), regarding *Icerya purchasi*,
he wrote me as follows :—

"For the last three years I have had a colony of
I. purchasi in a lemon tree in my garden : the other
day, being desirous of obtaining some living specimens,
I found that every one had been destroyed ; . . . . this
has been the result of two parasites. First the larva of
one of our native *Coccinellidæ*, but the principal exterminator has been a dipterous insect in the shape of a
minute, metallic, greenish black fly."

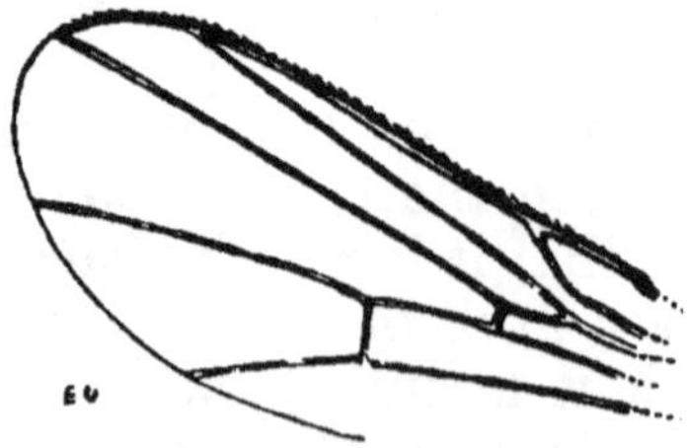

Fig. 32.—Portion of wing of South Australian dipterous parasite of
I. purchasi (since named by Dr. Williston *Lestophonus iceryæ*, gen. nov.).

A few specimens of this two-winged fly were sent over
to me, but they were too much injured by the journey,
or in unpacking, to be identified, and I could only
consequently give a few. rough notes of its general

appearance and a sketch of the neuration of a portion
of one wing.

Since then specimens reared by Mr. F. S. Crawford
have been forwarded to Prof. C. V. Riley, and at his
request been identified by Dr. S. W. Willeston as being
of a new genus and new species of the *Oscinidæ*, and
they have been named by him (descriptively of their
habits of killing or plundering the *Icerya*) *Lestophonus
Iceryæ.**

I have not yet seen a specimen or description of the
larva, but for general purposes the fly may be described
as about the sixteenth of an inch long, broadest across
the middle of the head, or in my specimens just behind
it, whence it gradually slopes off to the tail, so as to be
bluntly wedge-shaped when seen from above, and twice
the length of the widest part. Head with two large
compound eyes of a reddish colour, each occupying
about one-third of the width of the head, as seen from
above. The general colour or appearance dark greenish
black, or dark blue. The legs are stated by Dr. Willeston
to be rather short and strong, dark brown or blackish
brown ; front tarsi more lutescent or brownish yellow.

Those who wish full description, with good magnified
figure, are referred to Dr. Willeston's paper.

As this serviceable parasite has already been artificially
introduced into California, and further measures regarding it are now under consideration of the U. S. A.
Department of Agriculture, it may be hoped that means
will be discovered by which we also may be aided in
measures for serviceably reducing one at least of the
destructive insect-pests of South Africa.

Observation of Male Specimen of Icerya purchasi
from Natal.

On April 26th, this year, I was favoured by information from Mr. Richard J. Lewis, of Mount Park Crescent,

* See " An Australian Parasite of *Icerya purchasi*," by Dr. S. W.
Willeston, ' Insect Life,' No. 1, pp. 21, 22. Government Printing Office,
Washington.

H

Ealing, that amongst a number of specimens of *Icerya purchasi* received from Natal, about ten days previously, he had found a specimen of the male insect alive, and in fairly good condition. On comparing this with Prof. Riley's description of the American species, and also with his figure of the male insect in the U. S. A. Report, 1887, Mr. Lewis considered it agreed almost exactly excepting in some minor details as to colour and hairs, which might be easily explained by probable differences in method of examination or mounting.

Mr. Lewis was good enough to place in my hands a camera lucida drawing of the insect, coloured from life, and magnified to about 1½ inches in length ; and so far as I can judge (from comparison of this with Prof. Riley's figure) it appears to myself also to correspond minutely in wing-neuration, antennæ, and other essential points—all, in fact, which are represented.

I offer my best thanks to Mr. Lewis for his kind courtesy in permitting me to complete the observations of the South African *Icerya purchasi*, by publishing, before he does so himself in full, his interesting observation, which I believe to be the first recorded notice of the male of *Icerya purchasi* being found on the continent of Africa.—E. A. O.

Lecanium hesperidum, Linn.

Coccus hesperidum, Linn. Fauna Suecica, p. 264 ; Syst. Nat. i. 2, p. 739.

Calymnatus hesperidum, Costa, Nuov. Observ. 1835 ?,

Calypticus hesperidum, Costa, Faun. Ins. Nap. Gall-insect. 1837-8, 1 ; Lubbock, Proc. Roy. Soc. ix. 480 ; Beck, Trans. Roy. Micr. Soc. 1881, 47, &c.

Soft Orange Scale, or Broad Scale.*

Examples received from South Africa have been iden-tified by Mons. Signoret as belonging to this common

---

* I have not given a figure of this Scale, as it is too well known to require illustration.

and widely-distributed species, usually known under the popular name of the " Broad Scale." As the colour and form become considerably altered in dried specimens, which renders a description of such, imperfect and unsatisfactory, it has been considered more desirable to reprint the following description by Prof. Comstock, now of Cornell University, New York State, U. S. A., given in 1880 in his excellent report on Scale insects.

" *Adult female.*—Length 3—4 millm. Colour yellow, inclined to brown upon disk, often quite dark ; shape elongate-oval, nearly flat ; smooth and shining, with sparse punctures upon the disk ; after death the border above often becomes wrinkled radially for a narrow space. The antennæ are seven-jointed, the fourth and seventh subequal in length, and the third but little shorter ; first, second, fifth and sixth short and subequal. The legs are long and comparatively slender, with the tarsi shorter by one-fourth than the tibiæ ; the hair upon the trochanter is very long, and the tarsal claw is large ; the tarsal digitules are long and much widened at their extremities, and also stout at the base. The anal ring is very small, and is furnished with six long stout bristles."

" *Young larvæ.*—Long-oval ; antennæ with six joints only, of which the third is the longest."—Report of the Entomologist of the United States Department of Agriculture for 1880, p. 335. Washington, 1881.

This Scale, known in North America as the " Broad Scale," or " Soft Orange Scale," is very widely distributed geographically and also botanically. It is found in many parts of the world and on many kinds of plants. It is stated by Prof. Comstock to be found in N. America on Ivies, Oranges, and other plants ; in California it is recorded as found in nearly every locality where Citrus trees are grown, and that it infests the wood, foliage and fruit.

Mr. Maskell, in his 'Account of Insects noxious to Agriculture and Plants in New Zealand,' describes this

L. hesperidum, Linn., under the name of the "Holly and Ivy Scale," and records it as being present " everywhere on Ivy, Holly, Camellia, Orange, Laurel, Myrtle, Box, and many other plants out of doors or in greenhouses. In Europe chiefly on Ivy and Oranges, but frequently on other plants. In America on many plants."

In Europe this species of Scale insect is mentioned by M. Signoret as being found on Oranges, both in the greenhouse and the open air, and on surrounding plants.

The prevalence of this Scale on various kinds of plants might perhaps be turned to some little account in preventive measures, by clearing those found to foster it from the neighbourhood of where Orange trees are grown in only small numbers,—where they are grown in plantations this point would perhaps not make much difference.

The female insect, when full grown, may be generally described as an oval Scale, rather more than a twelfth of an inch in length, dark brown in colour above, lighter at the margin. It is considered to produce its young alive, and as many as forty-five have been found under one mother Scale.

The male Scale, as far as I am aware, has not been observed, or rather not so completely observed as to be certainly identified; but in the short paper on this insect given by the late Matthew Cooke, he mentions that in September, 1880, whilst preparing a mounting of an example of *Lecanium hesperidum* for microscopic use, an insect was observed coming from under a specimen beneath the glass, which finally released itself and proved to be a male Scale. I append part of the description and Mr. Cooke's comment below.*

* *Description.*—"Colour : body immaculate golden-yellow ; eyes dark or black ; antennæ (from the peculiar position in which they are placed I can only count seven joints) golden-yellow and hairy ; legs golden-yellow. As it did not agree with the description of any of the male Scale insects I had read of, or specimens of males of *aurantii, perniciosus, perseæ, rapax, roseæ,* or *purchasi* in my possession, I could only imagine

The injury which is caused by this Orange Scale is, firstly, by the Scale insects drawing away the juices of the leaves (or whatever part they attack) with their suckers, by which they waste the sap and also injure the state of the tissues by pricking them with numbers of little holes ; and, secondly, by the shoots (if badly attacked) becoming covered with masses of black filth.

In the case of some Scale-infested Orange or Lemon shoots sent over to me from California for examination, they were fairly smothered in the masses of Scales and black dirt. It is thus described in a short, clear, and spirited paper by Prof. MacOwan, Director of the Cape Town Botanic Gardens, on " Diseases of Orange Trees, Scale, &c."* :—

" When the Scale is only moderately present the tree keeps a-head of the injury, but if there be much of it, so that the Coccus' sugary excrement varnishes over the leaves, then there will come a detestable black fungus (*Capnodium Footii*), growing on the saccharine secretion and choking up the stomata or breathing-pores of the leaves. Now for this plague there is nothing to be done but cleaning down with alkaline and soapy syringings."

With regard to applications, probably any soapy or other wash would answer the purpose which would stifle or kill the Scales, without risk of damage to the leafage or fruit beyond what might be prevented by a " swilling" with clean water afterwards.

At pp. 79—86, in the preceding paper on Australian Bug or Soft Cushiony Scale, are various recipes which

---

that it was the male of *L. hesperidum* (be what it may it came from under the *L. hesperidum* Scale, and I fortunately preserved the mounting."— 'Injurious Insects of the Orchard, Vineyard, &c.,' by Matthew Cooke, late Chief Executive Horticultural Officer of California (Sacramento, Cal. U.S.A. 1883), pp. 164, 165.

* Paper on " Diseases of Orange Trees, the Scale, &c.," by Prof. P. MacOwan, F.L.S., Director of the Cape Town Botanic Gardens ; in 'Agricultural Journal,' published by the Department of Agriculture of the Cape Colony, No. 14, 1888, pp. 1, 2.

appear applicable also to this kind, and likewise a
recipe for a soft-soap and paraffin mixture found useful
for ordinary Scale insects, with directions for use.   But
whatever is used, the chance of success depends much
on the method of application : I therefore take leave to
give the remainder of Prof. MacOwan's advice on this
subject, in his own words (from the paper above quoted),
as it could not be more clearly and strongly conveyed,
and I would particularly draw attention to the good
advice given in italics :—

"A powerful syringe, or rather force-pump, with a
portable reservoir, is used to swish every part of the
foliage *from the inside.*   After the soap-lye has been on
the tree for 24 hours in dry, or say 36 hours in cool
damp weather, the syringing is repeated with plain
water, to get rid of both soap and the dead Scale insects.
If the water is as hot as the hand can bear, say 95° to
100°, it will be all the better.   By this means, perse-
veringly kept up, Mr. W. W. Dickson, of Ceres Road,
starting with a plantation of neglected trees, covered
with Scale, soon got them all as clean as the palm of
my hand, and good growth followed straight away.   Now
as to the wash.   For a first application, supposing Scale
to be badly developed, take 4 lbs. soft-soap and a full
quart of paraffin oil ; rub into the soap, little by little,
a gallon of hot water, and, when emulsionised into a
uniform oily mass, add the oil the same way.   Dilute
this down for use with nine gallons of warm water,
and keep thoroughly mixed while using with the force-
pump.

" Mr. Dickson used the soapy liquor of the wool-wash,
and thus utilised an otherwise useless lye-product.   For
a subsequent application the lye may be somewhat
weaker.   A good force-pump mounted on a barrel to
hold the lye, or the subsequent wash-water, may cost
£3 or £4, and is worth every penny of the money.   The
delivery hose should be mounted on a tube 3½ or 4 feet
long, and the labourer, dressed in a sack with holes for
head and arms, gets up *inside* the spread of the tree, if

it be large, and with the pump going *swishes the back of the leaves,—i. e.,* takes the enemy in the rear. *It is next to useless to spray the tree from the outside.* *

ORDER ARACHNIDA.

DIVISION ACARINA.

FAM. IXODIDÆ.

AMBLYOMMA HEBRÆUM, Koch. (Fig. 32.)

Amblyomma hebræum, Koch, Arachnidensys. iv. p. 63, t. 10, f. 36.

Cattle Ticks. "Shell Tick."

Together with the specimens of South African insects forwarded to me by Mr. Bairstow, he also sent samples of Cattle Ticks, known respectively as the "Great Cattle Tick" and the "Shell Tick, which, although very different in appearance, were considered on investigation to be male and female of one species.

Of these Mr. Janson wrote me as follows:—

"As regards the Ticks I have two specimens, a small one labelled "Shell Tick, Port Elizabeth,"† attached to a portion of skin, and a large one called the Great Cattle Tick: these I have not the slightest doubt, judging by allied species, are male and female of *Amblyomma hebræum* (Koch). The male is described and figured in the 'Ubersicht des Arachnidensystems,' by Koch, but the female, as far as I can find, has not been described."

"In the male of this species" (that is, in the kind called by Mr. Bairstow the Shell Tick, figured above life size and magnified—E. A. O.) the body is nearly flat and of a short ovate form, the broadest part behind; it

* Paper by Prof. MacOwan, above quoted.
† I have received several of this sex from Bedford, South Africa, but no females.

is of a pale greenish or slaty grey colour, usually darker or more or less shaded with red towards the sides; the spots and markings are red-brown or pitchy black; the hinder margin is crenulate, and there is an impressed submarginal line; the sides are sparsely punctured, and there are two small deep impressions in front; the palpi and legs are of a rust-red colour, the latter with a yellow spot at the ends of the joints; the length of the body is 6 millm."

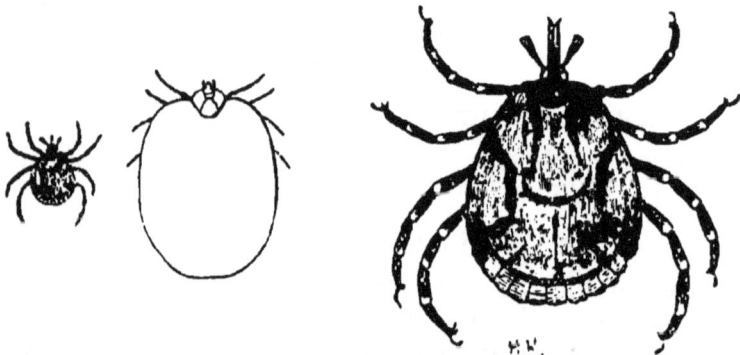

Fig. 32.—*Amblyomma hebræum*, male, life-size and magnified; outline figure showing size of female, inflated.

" In the female specimen " received (that is, the specimen sent by Mr. Bairstow under the name of the Great Cattle Tick, of which the size is given in the figure in outline—E. A. O.) " the body is enormously distended, and now of a dark brown-red colour, with a pale reddish grey spot in front; the surface is finely granulated, and when magnified is seen to be very finely striated; the legs are of the same colour, and marked as in the male. The length of the body is 22 millm."*
—O. E. J.

* The above is given merely as a general description. Those who desire a fuller description of *Amblyomma hebræum* (male), the Shell Tick of Port Elizabeth, will find it in the 'Arachnidensystems' of Koch, above referred to. With regard to the female, or Great Cattle Tick, the colour of the body cannot be given with precision, as in all probability it alters after death and immersion in spirit. In his notes Mr. Bairstow (casually) alludes to a great Cattle Tick, under the name of the " Blue

The first-mentioned of the above, which was sent over in spirit still adhering firmly to a piece of hide, and so remained during the time it continued in my possession, Mr. Bairstow described as " The disastrous hide-perforator of these regions commonly known here as the Shell Tick," very beautiful in appearance, but none the less injurious, as when its lancet sucker is inserted it remains in position for such a lengthened period as to cause evident distress to the victim and injury to the animal; also that it would indeed be a boon to the country if any means could be discovered to destroy— or, what would be better, prevent—the presence of a little creature which moves a market downwards at a high percentage."

With regard to the Great Cattle Tick, Mr. Bairstow forwarded a specimen with a quantity of eggs in spirits, and an outline, of somewhat oval form, three-quarters of an inch long by three eighths wide, giving the size of the parent Tick when it reached him, with eggs in thousands. It is interesting as pointing out such a vast prolific tendency. It lived a month after it commenced to deposit.

Excepting the great amount of mischief caused by these Ticks very little is noted of their habits, and therefore the following extract (appended in Murray's 'Aptera,' pp. 201—203, to the mention of *Amblyomma rotundatum*, Koch, of S. America) may probably be of service as giving an account of the general method of

Tick," as follows :—"The common huge Blue Tick, though sometimes occurring almost gregariously in thousands upon one beast, gorges to so filthy a repletion that it falls off upon the ground. The Shell Tick is left, though preceding the other in arrival." It appears, from the notes, that the "Blue Tick" and the "Great Cattle Tick" are most likely merely different common names for the same kind, therefore I have above drawn attention to the colour of the Great Cattle Tick as received having probably undergone the change which may be (to give a common example) seen in this country in Dog Ticks ; but, however this point may be, in the letterpress above I have only referred to the kinds sent over as "Shell Tick" and as "Great Cattle Tick," not at all to the Blue Tick, so, whether this is or is not the same as the Great Cattle Tick, this makes no confusion with identification of the others.—E. A. O.

life of the Ticks of this genus (*Amblyomma*), including the very serious harm caused by them to the infested cattle :—

"This (*A. rotundatum*) may be taken as the type of a multitude of Ticks that infest South America, where they are known by the name of Carapato, being so called in consequence of their resemblance to the Ricinus which bears that name in Portuguese.

"There are many species that go by this name, but no doubt the majority belong to the genus *Amblyomma*. They are common in all parts of South America where cattle abound, and they not only attack cattle, but also horses, dogs, and sheep, and occasionally man himself. Like our own Ticks they are found on plants, and when cattle become infested with them it is generally after feeding on open and exposed pastures, where the sun's heat is great, and they increase most in dry seasons.

"It is remarkable that cattle feeding in shady pastures and coppices are frequently quite free from the Carapato, but will acquire it by infection from others. The mode in which it appears to cause destruction to the animal infested by it is by the incessant irritation, which prevents the animal feeding or resting, and in consequence it becomes worn out. Many thousand head of cattle are annually carried off by them, and even a scarcity of food has been caused by them. Prof. Busk, from whom we take some of these details, in describing the young of one species (Trans. Mic. Soc., vol. i.), and the mischief that they do, mentions that 'they first appear on those parts of the skin uncovered by hair, and are then not larger than a pin's head, and make the part quite black by their numbers. They adhere so closely that scraping them off would tear off the skin. In a short time they increase to the size of a bean, or Common Tick, as seen in dogs, and fix themselves promiscuously on all parts of the hide, where covered with hair.'

"The same species appears to insinuate itself, in its incipient state, upon the human body, but is not known to assume the Tick form there (doubtless because not allowed to remain). They adhere most tenaciously to the skin, and, he says, 'they are believed to introduce themselves below it, and are very harassing, and even create soreness and inflammation. They generally affect persons who have been passing through woods, although not often seen or found on trees or plants.'

"Cuvier, after noting that 'they are found in thick woods abounding in brushwood, briars, &c.,' states that they attach themselves to low plants by the two fore legs, extending the other feet so as to seize anything that brushes against them, and, their claws being provided with caruncles that act as suckers, the slightest touch is sufficient to give them a hold.

"Besides fastening upon dogs, cows, horses, and other quadrupeds, they even lay hold of the tortoise, burying their suckers so completely in its flesh that they can hardly be detached by force and by tearing away the portion of skin to which they are fastened. They deposit a prodigious number of eggs."

The regular treatment for Tick on infested cattle is commonly well known to cattle-owners, but it may be remarked that tearing the creature away, or trying to do so, is apt to cause a deal of mischief. Unless some treatment is applied to make it lose hold the creature often breaks off, and the part by which it was attached remaining in the skin is very likely to cause a sore.

In a letter of Mr. Bairstow's dated Sept. 1, 1886, he mentions that Messrs. McDougall's dressing (presumably Dip or Smear) "is a capital thing for cleansing, and certainly drives Tick away." Also in a communication sent over by Mr. Bairstow, on Dec. 24th of the same year, from Mr. H. Mapplebeck, Premier Judge of Dogs and Poultry at the Agricultural Show held shortly before at Port Elizabeth, Mr. Mapplebeck mentions McDougall's "preparations" as what every S. African farmer should have in his possession, so that they are presumably of tried service: but for cases of this sort, if there is any difficulty, probably a letter to the Editor of that useful publication, the 'Agricultural Journal,' published by the Agricultural Department, Cape Colony,* would, in this and many other instances, secure a practical reply meeting all needs.

South American " Garrapatas."

Whilst the above observations on the South African Shell and Cattle Ticks were still in press, I was favoured with the following information (from personal observation) of habits and means of prevention of some of the South American Cattle Ticks, by Mr. C. P. Hayward, of the firm of Messrs. Tomlinson and Hayward, of Lincoln.

The specimens accompanying appeared on examination to be a species of *Hæmaphysalis;* and the description of the habits and some points of the history of these Garrapatas or Ticks, also the serious nature of the injuries inflicted and the means by which they may be checked, appear to me of so much practical service that I give them, by permission, in Mr. Hayward's own words :—

"As regards the treatment of these pests by us, we have had to deal with thousands of animals (cattle) infested with them, and to begin at the onset when the animals are first attacked. I will relate to you my own experience of a trip from Buenos Aires to the large Cattle Estancia of Señor Don Mariano Unzue, situated midway between the towns of Gualaguaychu and Conception del Uruguay in Entre Rios.

"Hearing that S. D. M. U. was losing some twenty-five to thirty animals *per day* through the pest of *Garrapatas* (this is the correct way of spelling this word by the natives of Buenos Aires), I proceeded to the estancia (farm), where I found the news too true, and the poor animals in a fearful state of emaciation.

"There were some 50,000 head of cattle on the estancia ; and not having had rain for some time the ground was hard, the grass parched up, and but little for them to eat, and, like many other pests, these Garrapatas appear associated with the poverty of the animals they live upon. The origin of these pests I could not gather correctly, but the natives told me that they first come in the long coarse grasses so prevalent there, and begin by attacking the legs of the cattle first, then the shoulder, and afterwards all over, and, like the Sheep Tick, are blood-suckers, but more tenacious than the Tick, as the Garrapata has always his head or sucker embedded firmly in the skin, and does not migrate among the hair of the cattle like the tick in the wool of the sheep. The Garrapata varies in size from the size of a pea to that of a *large* bean, and is, in its natural state, of a light greenish colour; those sent you have been that colour, but changed to their present colour through the spirit they are in, and which is no criterion of their natural state : it attacks horses, dogs, and even men, and to release them is most difficult, as their proboscis is left in if you attempt to *pull* them off, and causes great irritation ; the native, alive to the consequences, generally burns what is left exposed, *i. e.* the body, with a hot cigarette or cigar, and this seems to cause the Garrapata to relinquish its hold immediately.

"Our *modus operandi* has been to secure the animal and pour a solution of our *glycerine wash*, in the proportion of 1 part wash to 20 parts water, by means of a watering tin (as shown in the illustration sent you), when in less than five minutes all the Garrapatas have been killed, the effect of our wash having an *outward* destructive power upon them, as the solution simply paralyses the parasite, it being of a strong carbolic nature, and thus acts immediately upon the breathing-pores of the Garrapata. To treat the animals thus affected in South Africa we should urge the same process, which is by no means an expensive one on a large scale, where several hundreds or thousands of animals have to be treated : of course in South America the native uses the lassoo, and I have had as many as thirty men catching and throwing the animals for the process of pouring the solution upon them. For Africa no doubt they have a similar way of treating cattle, and having them in subjection when they require to handle them closely.

"The specimens of Garrapatas sent you are in their various stages of growth, and I would particularly call your attention to the smaller ones, and the group of three which I found—as all young ones are found—adhering close to the *head* of the full-grown ones, as if learning the art of blood-sucking. I must not forget to mention that the deaths of the animals occurred through the loss of blood these Garrapatas extract."*

In the above notes the point of the belief of the natives that the Ticks are picked up by the cattle in the long grass is well worth notice, as this is confirmed by observations of habits of Ticks elsewhere; and the points also of young Ticks being found near the adult specimens on the infested animal is of serviceable interest as pointing to multiplication taking place on the cattle, as well as the likelihood of the attack being picked up as above is worth notice, more particularly as this is confirmed by observations of habits of Ticks elsewhere.

The evidence given both by Mr. Hayward and previous scientific observers in South America, and by Mr. Bairstow in South Africa, as to the serious damage caused by these blood-sucking pests to the cattle, show the attack to be one deserving care both by remedial applications and also possible measures of cleanliness, and attention being given to "prevent overstocking on large cattle farms, by the long grasses being burnt that shelter the Ticks, and altogether giving greater attention to the condition of the localities of pasturage of the cattle, when such pests would be less numerous, if not wholly prevented."

* Extract from letter of March 29th, 1889, from Mr. C. P. Hayward to myself, on the subject of Cattle Ticks and methods of prevention.— E. A. O.

LIST OF INSECTS
FORWARDED FROM SOUTH AFRICA.

(Where an asterisk is appended the name only is given.)

Order COLEOPTERA.   Beetles.

Fam. MELOLONTHIDÆ.

Eriesthes stigmatica, Billb.   Mealie Chafer.
Hypopholis sommeri, Burm.   Vine Cockchafer.

Fam. DYNASTIDÆ.

Heteronychus arator, Fab.   "Keever Beetle."
Pentodon nireus, Burm.   Corn Chafers.
„ *contractus*, Bohm.

Fam. CETONIIDÆ.

Rhabdotis semipunctata, Fab.   Fruit Chafer.

Fam. ANOBIIDÆ.

Anobium paniceum, Linn.   "Boot Beetle"; Paste Beetle.

Fam. BOSTRICHIDÆ.

Apate Francisca, Fab.*

Fam. TENEBRIONIDÆ.

Psammodes obliquatus, Sol.   Mealie Beetle.
Opatrum micans, Germ.   Carrot and Potato Beetle.

Fam. CANTHARIDÆ.

Mylabris oculata, Thunb.   Blister Beetles injurious to vegetation.
„ *lunata*, Pall.   „   „   „
„ *16-guttata*, Thunb.*   „   „   „
„ *capensis*, Linn.*   „   „   „
„ *grœndali*, Billb.*   „   „   „
„ *undata*, Thunb.*   „   „   „
Lytta pallidipennis, Haag.* |„   „   „

Fam. BRUCHIDÆ.

Bruchus sp. ? (*subarmatus*, Gyll.?).   Bean-seed Bruchus.

Fam. OTIORHYNCHIDÆ,

Phlyctinus inæqualis, Bohm.*

Fam. PRIONIDÆ.

Erioderus hirtus, Fab.*
Macrotoma dimidiaticornis, Waterh.*

Fam. CERAMBYCIDÆ.

Litopus dispar, Thoms.*
Promeces linearis, Linn.*
Hypocrites mendax, Fahr.*

Fam. LAMIIDÆ.

Phryneta spinator, Fab.*
Ceroplesis bicincta, Fab.   Willow or Timber Longhorn Beetles.
  „   *hottentotta*, Fab. „   „   „   „
Alphitopola maculosa, Pasc. Orange-tree   „   „

Fam. GALERUCIDÆ.

Iphidea capensis, Baly, n. sp.   Fruit-tree Iphidea.

Fam. HALTICIDÆ.

Dibolia intermedia, Baly.   Dark blue Flea-Beetle.

Fam. COCCINELLIDÆ.

Rodolia Iceryæ, Janson.   Ladybird, feeder on Australian Bug.

Order HYMENOPTERA.   Wasps, Ants, &c.
Fam. PONERIDÆ.

Streblognathus Æthiopicus, Smith.*

Fam. FORMICIDÆ.

Camponotus fulvopilosus, Deg.*

Order LEPIDOPTERA.   Butterflies and Moths.
Fam. PAPILIONIDÆ.

Papilio demoleus, Linn.   Orange Butterfly.

Fam. SPHINGIDÆ.

Acherontia Atropos, Linn.   Death's Head Moth.

Fam. BOMBYCIDÆ.

Trilocha ficicola (Westwood).   Fig Moth.

Fam. TINEIDÆ.

Plutella cruciferarum, Zell.   Diamond-back Moth.

Order DIPTERA.   Two-winged Flies.
Fam. MUSCIDÆ.

Ceratitis citriperda, Macl.   Orange Fly: "Trypeta Fly," S.A.

Fam. HIPPOBOSCIDÆ.

Hippobosca Struthionis, Janson, n. sp.   Ostrich Fly.
Olfersia spinifera, Leech.   Pigeon Fly.

Order NEUROPTERA. Dragonflies, &c.
Fam. TERMITIDÆ.
Termes angustatus, Ramb.*

Fam. HEMEROBIIDÆ.
Chrysopa (iceryæ, n. sp.). Lace-wing Fly.

Order ORTHOPTERA. Locusts, Crickets, &c.
Fam. ACRIDIIDÆ.
Phymateus morbillosus, Linn. Variable Locust.
Cyrtacanthacris ruficornis, Fab. Red-horned Locust.

Order RHYNCHOTA. Aphides, Scale Insects, &c.
Fam. CERCOPIDÆ.
Ptyelus grossus, Fab. Tree Froghopper.

Fam. COCCIDÆ.
Icerya Purchasi, Maskell. Australian Bug; Cottony Cushion Scale.
Lecanium Hesperidum, Linn. Broad Scale.

Class ARACHNIDA.—Order ACARINA.
Fam. IXODIDÆ.
Amblyomma hebræum, Koch. Shell Tick: Great Cattle Tick.

INDEX.

Acherontia atropos, 40

Agricultural Journal of Cape Colony, where procurable, Preface

Alphitopola maculosa, 32

Amblyomma hebræum, 103—107

Anobium paniceum, 14—17 (see "Boot Beetle")

"Australian Bug": appearance of in S. Africa, 70; description of, 72—79; methods of prevention and remedy, 79—90; soft-soap washes, to destroy, 80—85; hand-picking, and shaking down to destroy, 87—89; danger of spreading, 90; list of applications used to destroy, 90; insect destroyers of, 91—97; observation of male of, 97

Bean Bruchus, 22—28; description of beans infested by, 25; grub furnished with three pairs of foot-like appendages, 26; to destroy in infested beans, 26, 27; Calvert's Carbolic Acid, McDougall's Sewage Carbolic, and Blue Vitriol, useful to destroy infestation, 27; fumigation by bisulphide of carbon, 27; how to distinguish infested beans, 28; change of crop as a means of prevention, 28; measures of prevention and remedy, 26—28

Bean-seed Beetle, 22—28

Bisulphide of carbon to poison insects in seeds, 27

Blister Beetles, 21, 22

Blue Vitriol for dressing infested bean-seed, 27

Boot Beetle, 14—17; allied to English Death-watch Beetle, 15; method of injury, 15; to boots at Port Elizabeth and Cape Town, exported from England, 15, 16; method of life of, 16; suggestion of means of prevention for, 17

Bruchus sp.? (subarmatus, *Gyll.?*), 22

Calvert's Carbolic Acid, useful for dressing beans infested by Beetle, 27

Carrot-root and Potato-leaf Beetle, 19, 20

Ceratitis citriperda, 49

Ceroplesis bicincta, 29
„   hottentotta, 31

Chafers, to destroy, by shaking down, 4; by catching with nets, 14; grubs, sometimes at roots of grass, 5; grubs, to turn out from roots, 4; kind of information needed regarding methods to destroy, 5

Chrysopa (? iceryæ, n. sp.), destructive to Australian Bug, 93—96; description of larva (or maggot) of, 94

Coccinella (Ladybird Beetle) destructive to Australian Bug, 91

Cyrtacanthacris ruficornis, 65

Death's-head Moth, 40—43; same species as the British kind, 41; fond of honey, 41; caterpillars feed on vine-leaves, 42; got rid of by hand-picking, 43

Diamond-back Moth, 46—49; caterpillars of, attack cabbage, 47; means of prevention for, 48, 49
Dibolia intermedia, 35

Eriesthis stigmatica, 1
Erioderus hirtus, 33

Fig Moth, 43—46; injurious to leafage and buds, 45; remedies, 46
Flea Beetle, dark blue, 35—37: reported to be seen in great numbers in British Caffraria about 1883, 36
Froghopper, Tree, 65—68
Fruit blossom, Blister Beetles injurious to, 21, 22
Fruit Chafer, 12—14; nearly allied to English Rose Chafer, 13
Fruit-tree Iphidea, 34

" Garrapatas," South American Ticks, 108—110; habits of, 109; Glycerine wash of Messrs. Tomlinson & Hayward destructive to, 109; method for applying on a large scale, 109
Glanville, Miss, Preface

Heteronychus arator, 5
Hippobosca equina, 59
    ,,   rufipes, 57
    ,,   struthionis, 56—60
Hypocrites mendax, 34
Hypopholis sommeri, 2

Icerya purchasi, 69—98 (see "Australian Bug")
Insects, list of species sent from S. Africa, 111—113
Iphidea capensis, 34

" Keever " Beetle, 5—9; said to feed on wheat-roots, 6; also on potatoes, 7; found in neighbourhood of grass land, 8; fly about trees on hot nights, 8; manure suggested as means of trapping, 7—9.

Lace-wing Fly ("Golden-eye") destructive to Australian Bug, 93—96
Lecanium hesperidum, 98—103
Lestophonus iceryæ, 96, 97
Litopus dispar, 34
Locust (variable), 62—65
Lytta pallidipennis, 21

McDougall's Sewage Carbolic, for dressing beans infested by Beetle, 27
Macrotoma dimidiaticornis, 33
Mealie Beetles, 1, 18
Mylabridæ, injurious to peas, fruit blossom, &c., 21, 22
Mylabris lunata, 21, 22
    ,,   oculata, 21, 22
    ,,   sp. of mentioned, namely capensis, grœndali, 16-guttata, and undata, 21

Olfersia spinifera, 61
Opatrum hadroides (in St. Helena),   ,,   micans, 19   [20
Orange Butterfly, 37—40; common in Eastern province, 40; caterpillar infests fennel and orange leaves, 40; hand-picking caterpillars and turning soil round roots of trees, to prevent attack of, 40
Orange Fly, 49—56; localities of, 50; fruits that the caterpillars of feed on, 51—53; to preserve fruit from, 54
Orange Scale, Soft, 98—103; localities of, 99; specimen of supposed male of, 100; soft-soap and paraffin wash, to destroy, 101; method of application, 102; dress for operator, 102
Orange tree, Longhorn Beetle of, 32
Ostrich Fly, 56—60; numerous on ostriches observed, 58; does not lay eggs, 59; suggestions of remedies for, 59, 60

Papilio demoleus, 37
Paste Beetle, 14 (see " Boot Beetle ")

Peas and beans, Blister Beetles injurious to, 21, 22
Pentodon contractus, 11
,, nireus, 10
Phryneta spinator, 33
Phymateus morbillosus, 62
Pigeon Fly, 61, 62
Plutella cruciferarum, 46
Potato-leaf and Carrot-root Beetle, 20; allied species found in potato-grounds and on ploughed fields in St. Helena, 20
Prevention and remedy, measures of : for caterpillars turning soil round stems of infested trees, 40; shaking does not answer where caterpillars have clinging powers, 46; hand-picking, 40, 43; sheep driving, 49; chrysalis cocoons, turning out from the ground, 43; picking off trees, 46; burning, on remains of infested crop or weed plants, 48; burying down, 48; shaking down moths, 46 (jarring trees so as to shake off the infestation, and stirring the ground, is also serviceable for getting rid of Beetles or of their maggots below the surface of the earth); change of ground, 59; dressing infested ground with quicklime, &c., to kill bird pests, 59; clearing out harbouring places in stock or ostrich enclosures, 60; burning infested grass to destroy Tick, 110; for washes see references.
Promeces linearis, 34
Psammodes obliquatus, 18
Ptyelus grossus, 65

Rhabdotis semipunctata, 11
Rodolia iceryæ, 91—93; introduction of into New Zealand to destroy Australian Bug, Preface

Scale, Cottony Cushion, 69—98
,, Orange, 98—103
Shell Tick, 103—107; female of, known as Great Cattle Tick, 104; McDougall's dressing, good application for, 107

Tarred bands, to prevent passage of wingless insects, 88, 89
Ticks (Cattle) South African and South American, 103 — 110; McDougall's Smear, and Tomlinson and Hayward's Glycerine Wash, useful to destroy, 107, 109; preventive measures, 110
Tobacco, with soft-soap wash, 81
Tree Froghopper, 65—68
Trilocha ficicola, 43
Trypeta Fly, 49—56

Vine Chafer, 2—5

Washes, glycerine, 109; ostrich droppings boiled in water, 86; soft-soap, 80—85; to dissolve sulphur in, 81; whale-oil soap and sulphide of soda, 82; method of mixing soft-soap and mineral oil in U.S.A., 83, 84; soft-soap and paraffin, as used by Mr. Ward of Stoke Edith, 84; as used by Mr. Malcolm Dunn of Dalkeith, 84—86
Wheat Chafers, 5—9; 10, 11
Willow Beetles, 29 — 32; very common and injurious, 32

WEST, NEWMAN AND CO., PRINTERS, HATTON GARDEN, E.C.